POTENTIAL

The **5TH** P of Leadership

UNLEASH YOUR FUTURE

I0503855

RAKESH MEHROTRA

INDIA • SINGAPORE • MALAYSIA

Notion Press Media Pvt Ltd

No. 50, Chettiyar Agaram Main Road,
Vanagaram, Chennai, Tamil Nadu – 600 095

First Published by Notion Press 2021
Copyright © Rakesh Mehrotra 2021
All Rights Reserved

ISBN 978-1-68538-964-2

Dedication

I dedicate this book to my beloved wife, who always brought out the best in me, but in her unique way. My unsolicited advice to her would invariably fall on deaf ears. I would be forced to remind her that as a person running a consulting company, organizations paid for my advice and implemented solutions suggested by me.

Her consistent response was that your corporate solutions don't work in the house and if you have something unique to say why don't you write a book? This was her way of encouraging me to share with others, what I have learned over 43 years of my work experience.

I began writing this book towards the latter part of 2018 and was moving ahead at a decent pace till our company picked up a very large order that kept us working 10 hours a day for over a year and the book was forgotten.

2020 was the year of lockdown and we savored the break. Things did pick up later that year but by April 2021 organizations got busy with their plans for the current financial year. I was again raving and ranting about there being no work when she reminded me about the unfinished book. I pulled out the material and realized that what I had written still made sense after a gap of three years. I started devoting a couple of hours a day to completing this assignment.

In the last week of April 2021, I returned from Delhi to Goa just in time to beat the second lock-down, without realizing that I was infected by the COVID-19 virus. Soon after I was hospitalized and my wife followed me to the hospital three days later. Our 37 years of partnership ended when on the second day in the ICU she gave up her fight with the dreaded virus just so she could watch over me.

Right through my stay in the hospital, I could feel her presence and I committed to myself to complete the book at the earliest, for her sake. I scraped through the ordeal and was discharged after 17 days in the hospital, of which 10 days were spent in the ICU.

What encouraged me to complete this book was her confidence, that I do have a different perspective on leadership, which I need to share with the world.

Contents

My Journey

I was born in 1957. Though there is nothing spectacular about that year to the best of my knowledge, it did put me in the right place at the right time to attempt writing a book on what constitutes Leadership Potential. It made me just the right age to be a part of the few revolutions that shaped corporate India a couple of decades later.

I am writing about my work experience just to share the exposure I have had over the four decades of my career; how it equipped me to write about "Leadership Potential" and why I formed, what I believe, is a perspective quite different from most of the leaders I come across.

The first corporate revolution was the office automation revolution that started around 1975. These were exciting times as electronic typewriters and photocopiers were being introduced in the market for the first time (computers were still some time away). There were plenty of organizations willing to shell out huge sums of money for acquiring these efficiency tools. Before that, the only technology visible in offices were manual typewriters and mechanical cyclostyling machines to laboriously create copies of a master document. There was, however, no option of photocopying documents. I was, then, also a part of the action when the Insurance and ITES revolutions took place in 2000.

There were, of course, other corporate revolutions happening too around the same time but since I had no part to play in them, I gained no learnings from them. Being a part of the ones mentioned above left me with huge learnings that serve me even today. There is always more learning if you join a start-up, in our case the industry itself was a start-up. It was all trial and error, analysis and back to trial and error. This shaped my style of working for the rest of my professional career.

Courtesy of the government's policy of charging exorbitant duties and not providing licenses to foreign manufactures, plus discouraging joint ventures from manufacturing in India, the office automation tools that we take for granted today could only be seen in Hollywood movies.

Slowly these products entered the country in a knockdown condition and were assembled by some blue-eyed corporates that had the blessing of the establishment.

It's around this time, in 1978, that I reached Mumbai after graduating from Kanpur University with a 62% in B com, (which incidentally is also the highest marks I ever scored), looking for a job – ANY JOB. I was hired by an addressing machine company that used steel plates to print out addresses, obviously, but could also print invoices and payrolls. I was appointed as an underling to a sales executive and tasks assigned to me included taking notes at meetings, carrying my senior's briefcase, and physically drawing the documents on chart papers which could then be printed on our machines and presented to clients as proof of the superiority of our system.

These machines provided a lot of clarity as people did not have to guess the numbers if some aspiring doctor was creating a pay sheet. Imagine the joy an employee would experience if an illegible 3 was mistaken for an 8 by the accountant while disbursing salaries. Our system prevented that from happening.

Either I was a fast learner or the industry was in the growth stage, as within a year I was promoted and transferred to Ahmedabad. Here, I was assigned my own underling to carry my briefcase and do all the heavy lifting while I tried to look important and knowledgeable. Life was beautiful and I could have carried on in this mode forever. However, a year later I resigned abruptly.

I had planned a road trip with three other friends. We were to ride on our rickety old Java motorcycles, from Mumbai (Bombay back then) to the Rohtang Pass and back. On the way back we were to stop at Chandigarh as we had been selected as "Marshals" for the first-ever Himalayan Rally. Two days before my departure, my sanctioned leave was cancelled, and no amount of reasoning and pleading made my manager change his mind.

The trip lasted 15 days and we were back in Mumbai. All my friends went back to their respective jobs but I had nowhere to go. One of my neighbours, who owned a factory gave me the brilliant idea of buying a transport vehicle and driving it myself initially. As the business grew, I could add on more vehicles and before I knew it I would have a flourishing transport business. I loved the idea and convinced my father to keep his house in Mumbai as surety (I was in sales, remember) for the Matador one tonner.

The reality on the road was very different from what we had planned. Though I was making more money than what a job paid me, it was still not enough to expand the business. Part of the problem was my financial indiscipline. I blew up in the evening what I earned during the day.

I was trying to figure out what to do when fate intervened. I had a serious accident on Juhu beach that made driving impossible for me for at least a year. So now I had no job, no source of income, and a bank loan to pay off. I was certain my father was going to throw me out of his house before the bank impounded it (while he could still claim it to be his). I got back to the corporate world and kept a driver with the only expectation of paying the bank EMI and his salary and anything else that he earned was also for him to keep.

I started again at the lowest rung as years of running my business were not counted as experience. My role involved selling more advanced equipment like electronic typewriters and photocopiers. Selling was easy in those days as there was hardly any competition, thanks to the policies of Nehru and Indira Gandhi.

Most of the sales were completed promptly after a little grovelling and begging on the part of the customer. The customer would request us to try to get them a better rate from our manager and to deliver the equipment within six months from the date of full payment. The first request was easily met as we had abundant margins, though we couldn't live up to the second one every time. I remember in 1984 a top-of-the-line photocopier from a prominent brand, with sorting and other facilities was being sold for INR 1,65,000. In the same amount of money, one could buy three Maruti 800 cars or two flats of 2BHK in a government housing scheme at the Juhu Versova Link Road.

This is also the time I got married to Patricia and was blessed with a son in 1985. We named him Siddharth Mark. As the financial burden increased, we decided that going to the Gulf for employment was a good option. Qatar Armed Forces were looking out for soldiers and I got selected for the job. At the age of 29, I left for Qatar leaving my wife and a four-month child behind. The purpose of this move was to make enough money to buy ourselves a house in Mumbai. There was no concept of home loans in those days unless one could provide a separate surety equal to the value of the loan. I didn't even try selling this idea to my father and quietly left for the Gulf.

My experience in Qatar – which included undergoing training as a soldier, from people whose language we did not understand, whose culture was alien to us and who did not even share the same motivations - changed me completely. This is the first time in my short career I had experienced great leadership and saw first-hand, the ability of leaders to transform a team, one member at a time.

The leaders I am referring to were our trainers who took charge of us the moment we landed in Qatar. The trainees in the group were from different countries, vastly different educational backgrounds, and most importantly different levels of physical fitness and commitment. Getting all these diverse characters on the same page, as effortlessly as they did, in a short span of six months is something that the corporate world can learn from.

I am sure the Indian Army does an equally great job or an even better one, but I have not had the privilege of experiencing their training. Though once on the job I did not see the same commitment from all the officers, but for people who wanted to learn from the experience, it was an opportunity of a lifetime.

I firmly believe that if India has to tap into its true potential, a one-year army conscription must be made mandatory after the 12th standard. Here, you build the character of the students and teach them skills that industry needs. In my opinion, our policy of granting dole to most people at the drop of a hat is making us lazy and is creating a burden on the system.

We were 60 recruits from India and were handed over to three trainers at the airport itself who herded us like cattle to our tents with clear instructions to be ready in our civilian clothing by 5:30am the next morning. Two days were consumed in completing the paperwork, issuing stores, and understanding the schedule.

On day three training started in earnest. Every morning at 5:30 am we would be running on sand dunes. I was a regular runner at Juhu beach so it worked fine for me. As far as I was concerned the beach had come to my tent. Plus, we had the privilege of watching the most exotic sunrise – day after day. 7:00 am to 8:00 am was a break for breakfast at the mess which was 3kms away. The one-hour break also involved getting back to our tents, changing into our overalls, and re-assembling on the Parade Ground. For the initial part of the training, the Indian contingent was kept intact, which was a relief.

Though I cover many leadership examples from the army in my training sessions, here I share just one to demonstrate how differently the corporate world and the army react to a similar situation.

Every army prides itself on the quality of the March Past that their soldiers perform, however, every individual does not have the same level of motor coordination. Invariably a couple of trainees would make mistakes as there is a lot of technique and timing required to perform even something as simple as a left turn. This situation is not very different from what we face in the corporate world when we induct new hires or when people perform at different levels on the floor and not everyone lives up to the expectations we have from them.

Before I share what the army trainers do in such a situation and the thought process behind their actions, I would request you to pause and think about how the corporate world would react in a similar scenario. I suggest you don't read ahead and visualize an actual scenario of a person who is a below-average performer during induction, training, or while on the shop floor. How does the corporate world handle this issue of under-performance?

In most teams, such employees would be singled out for more training or be handed over to HR to be put on a performance improvement plan. If over some time, the performance does not improve the person may be asked to leave and a replacement is found.

The army when faced with a similar situation uses a different strategy. Even if two people falter the entire group of 20 trainees is punished. The punishment would consist of ordering the trainees to touch the nearest tree and get back. The nearest tree in a desert could be half a kilometre away and with summer temperatures hovering around mid-40degree Celsius, it was a harsh punishment.

The trainer would, then, segregate the people into three groups. The first five trainees to get back from the run would be asked to perform 50 pushups, the next 10 would be allowed to rest in the shade, while the last five would be ordered to repeat the punishment. Please take another pause and try to figure out what the trainer is trying to achieve.

The first five did not get there accidentally, they ran very hard to be in the top 5. This group was also not static. There was tough competition to get into this group. The 50 pushups were not punishment but a recognition of their ability to do more. It was telling them that they were the best in the group and were capable of taking on bigger challenges. The next 10 were displaying acceptable levels of performance that would improve with time and the last 5 needed to buckle up. They needed more pushing hence were ordered to do another 1km run.

What did this differential treatment achieve? It made sure that everyone ran the best they could. The top 5 did not want to get dislodged from the elite group. For the people in the second group it was a matter of prestige to break into the top 5 group, so they gave it their best shot. The trainees who were in the last group that was made to repeat the punishment hated it and wanted to be part of the group that got to rest in the shade.

What would have happened if everyone was treated equally irrespective of their capability and commitment? The punishment would have become just that - a punishment to be endured, but there would be no incentive to push oneself and strive for improvement.

The trainees who made it most often into the top 5 were treated differently. They got all the meaty roles. The trainer would make one of them in charge if he had to step out or even while he was around. He also allowed them to take unsolicited breaks, besides giving other important assignments.

The meatiest role that the top 5 got to perform was collecting rations from the stores in the city. This involved going into town in a three-tonner to fetch rations for 3000 people. It was back-breaking work but came with its own set of privileges. One got to skip the monotony of training, got an opportunity to see the city and most importantly, on the way back one could consume whatever one wanted from the stores. No questions asked.

Though our training slots were from 8:00 am to 11:30 am and again from 3:00 pm to 5:00 pm, for the people who were struggling it was a busy day. Some person from the group was always busy training them and the learners were also eager to improve and put in extra effort as they knew they were the cause of the group's suffering. With just men around, you can imagine the language used and the threats issued. It was all taken in good spirit though and improved the bonding amongst the team members. The biggest advantage of punishing the group instead of the individual was that trainees took it upon themselves to get the stragglers trained and in the shortest duration.

I understand that one size does not fit all and that it is not possible to punish the entire group in the corporate space for the mistakes of a couple of individuals. Instead of punishment can we use reward as a motivator? Instead of recognizing and rewarding only the best performer, can we also reward those people who devote their time and energy in upskilling and supporting others? And what about your top talent? If you don't acknowledge them and treat them differently, won't they become mediocre in no time?

In the corporate world, I am sure a lot of top talent slowly starts performing below their capability simply because promotions and increments are based on tenure, qualifications and so many other factors. Not on performance, nor on the potential for taking on bigger responsibilities.

The army also taught us that most of the limitations that we impose on ourselves are not physical but are driven by the mind. Two months into the training, we started visiting the firing range for weapon training where we did target practice with rifles, heavy machine guns, and hand grenades. The equipment and the ammunition had to be carried by us to the firing range. The range was around 7kms away and the route was mostly over soft sand. We were bone-tired after the first few kms but kept going as there was no other option. After practice, we were driven back in trucks, but the day did not end there. We had to clean the equipment, reassemble it, get it inspected, and hand it over before we could crash for the day.

We assumed that the next day would be slightly lighter because of the physical ordeal of the previous day. However, the day started like any other and the training intensity did not diminish. Within 15 minutes of starting out though, all body aches and exhaustion were forgotten. The army teaches us to push to our ultimate limit and beyond. This learning has served me well in my professional and personal life.

One fine morning the Indians in the camp were asked to assemble at the parade ground. We were made a very simple offer. The Non-Muslims could either choose to convert to Islam, which would come along with many benefits, or be deported back to India. The leadership at our camp had changed and the new leadership was not so tolerant of non-Muslims working in the army. A week later 24 of us were deported back to India after completing three and a half years of our five-year contract.

I had accomplished my objective and by the time I got back to India, my wife and son had already moved into a two-bedroom flat in Lokhandwala, Andheri. I started doing the rounds of companies for a job and discovered that my experience in the office automation industry was not considered as there was a break and 3.5 years in the army was not 'relevant'. The choice of getting back to the corporate world and re-starting right at the bottom of the heap was not the one I wanted to take.

I was brimming with confidence as we had just bought ourselves a house, a new motorbike, and we still had a decent balance in the bank. I started looking around for a business opportunity. I realized that quite a few shops and restaurants were getting air-conditioned and most of them were using air curtains to prevent AC loss. This is the equipment that throws a strong draft of air vertically to separate the ac and non-ac areas in restaurants and shopping centres. Everywhere I went I noticed only National Air curtains. I learned that they were available for INR 20000/- and managed to buy a scrapped piece for INR 5000/-

I took this to a friend who had a small workshop with a lathe machine and we ripped the piece apart to understand the workings of the equipment. We decided to make a near copy of the machine, using only the best quality material in the prototype, with the understanding that we could scale down the quality of components selectively if the costing was going haywire. To our surprise after using that best quality material, accounting for labour cost, and keeping a buffer for hidden costs the equipment cost us only INR 4500/-. We tested it rigorously and it performed perfectly.

I hired two technically sound workers, who had worked on the prototype, and rented a table space in my friend's workshop. Though National had only one model, we made two more models with a stronger throw just in case people wanted a more powerful unit. The more presentable of the two workers was appointed as my part-time assistant and his job was to say "Yes Sir" to everything I said in front of the client and hold my briefcase so that I could look important and knowledgeable.

We still needed a strategy to sell the machines. We realized that most shop keepers contracted the air conditioning activity to the many assemblers who had mushroomed around the same time, who in turn offered air curtains as a part of the deal. We, therefore, decided to approach the contractors to do the selling for us so we could focus on manufacturing.

I loved the idea as it was mine, but I still threw it open for discussion as my team members knew as much as I about the equipment and the industry. They must have been trained very well by me to say "Yes Sir", as the only thing I heard from them during our brainstorming sessions was "Yes sir. It is a very good idea."

With a good product, generous margins to play around with, and steady demand in the market, what could possibly go wrong with our strategy?

Everything!

The first four contractors we visited to share our lucrative offer with, started pointing towards the door within the first 5 minutes, mistakenly assuming that we had got disoriented in their mingy two-room office and did not know the way out. They proceeded to dispatch us with undue haste when we did not take their hint. After the fourth encounter, it dawned on us that they already had such an agreement with National so why would they bother about us.

Next, we decided to approach the shop owners who were getting their premises air-conditioned, but they dismissed us. Why? Cause ensuring cooling efficiency was the contractor's job, they would not like to interfere with the contractor's work with an untested machine only to save a few thousand rupees.

So now we had a superior product that we were willing to sell at half the price of the competition but still no orders. However, what we did notice in our visits to all the shops was that in most cases the National air curtains were vibrating and making a noise. We knew that there was no issue with the equipment. It was just an uneven accumulation of dust on the rotor blades as these air curtains were not designed for the dusty conditions of the roadside shops in Mumbai.

The next plan was to provide servicing to existing National Air Curtains to generate some revenue. However, we decided that any machine that we serviced would have to carry a metallic sticker saying, "Maintained by Power Air Curtains". We designed the sticker in such a manner that one had to have perfect vision and had to be stationed right under the machine to read "Maintained by" while "Power Air Curtains" were visible from across the street.

We decided to service only those machines where we could put our sticker even if it meant walking away from the business. For this model to succeed we needed to get two things right. The sticker had to be attractive so no one could complain about the aesthetics of the machine being compromised. Two, we had to use the strongest adhesive available in the market! In the process of checking out every air-conditioned shop in different markets of Mumbai, we discovered that there were already two Indian companies that were making Air Curtains, but fortunately for us they provided no service to their customers.

At the end of the first month when we took stock of our reality, we realized that we were in a very happy situation. We had made a profit after accounting for salaries and expenses, one employee had been promoted and had become my assistant. We were hiring aggressively and our employee strength was going up from 2 to 5. We were also hunting for an industrial shed of our own to rent and we had received our first order for an Air Curtain.

In 1989, we adopted an eight-month baby girl, who grew up to be a strong-willed individual, outstanding in studies, and like our son, excellent in sports and athletics. We named her Gazal Kimberly. Life was beautiful. Weekdays were about work and studies, and on most weekends we headed out to an outdoor location or a resort.

The team worked very hard and the business grew from strength to strength over the next 6 years. After shops, we targeted the pharmaceutical industry where it is one of the GMPs to install air curtains in certain areas, cold storages, automobile paint shops, flight kitchens, and many more segments. We even installed Air Curtains in offices and celebrity homes. The business was growing, repeat orders and word of mouth business kept our production unit working at full capacity. Our focus on generating revenue from servicing did not diminish and we were open to servicing any brand of Air Curtains. During this period, we also bought a fancy office close to our residence so that the different teams did not have to operate from the factory anymore. Only the production guys went to the factory while others reported at the office.

That is when we decided to spend Holi with a close friend in Pune. We reached in time to attend a rocking party where a lot of people from the residential complex had also been invited. The next morning while I was still nursing a hangover Pat, my wife, stepped onto the balcony to enjoy the view. She called me to join her there as right below our balcony was a beautiful row house exactly like the one she had been eyeing in Mumbai, but which was way beyond our means. She had a green thumb, had grown up in a bungalow, and always wanted to live in one. She was convinced that this decision of moving to Pune is perfect for us. I thought it was a big decision and we needed to think it through. Later in the morning when we stepped out to play Holi and saw the facilities that the property offered, I was also convinced that this is the life we wanted to give our children. I had literally grown up at the BIC club in Kanpur, where we had facilities like a swimming pool, TT, Billiards, Squash. This township in Pune offered all these and more.

I borrowed money from my friend, paid the builder a token amount, and within three months the family shifted to Pune. I became a weekend husband (a weakened husband by some accounts). I would drive down post-lunch from Mumbai every Friday and would leave early Monday morning from Pune. This arrangement worked fine as I could give my undivided attention to work 5 days a week and had a vacation at a resort every weekend. However, I could maintain this discipline only for a few months, and slowly I started spending more time in Pune than initially planned while trying to monitor activities in Mumbai through landline connections as cell phones were still in the future.

It took 6 years to build the business and another 5 years to run it into the ground. It started with quality issues, irregular service, lost orders but the decline was so imperceptible that no alarm bells went off. In 1999 I discovered the company was in debt and I had no realistic plan for recovery. Selling off the office allowed me to clear my debts, pay off the employees their legal dues, and I was still left with some funds. We retained a house in Mumbai and I moved to Pune.

When the business was flourishing, I had bought a 9 seater Matador to cart our machines around. This was necessary to avoid harassment from the Excise Inspectors who could flag down any vehicle carrying commercial material. These guys were given unlimited powers. They would attach vehicles and seal factories at the drop of a hat even if a company was below the applicable limit for excise.

In Pune, while dropping our children off to school in the Matador I got flagged by many parents asking me if it was a school bus. In 2000, my new business was launched ferrying kids from 8 schools including one of the best schools in Pune where both our kids studied. Hats off to the culture of the school, driven primarily by the Principal, that there was never an awkward moment, either for the children or me. After two years I kept a driver as I wanted to do something more stimulating.

In 2000 I got a call from an ex-colleague, asking me to meet him at his office. He was one of the most sincere and driven salespeople I had known so I knew it would be something worthwhile. He had become a Manager at ICICI Prudential, selling life insurance, and wanted to enroll me as an Associate to sell policies for ICICI Prudential. On my off days and in the evenings, I started to sell insurance and did extremely well. While most people sold it as an investment or a tax-saving tool, I focused on the peace of mind it brought and as an essential step to being responsible parents. 20 years on I still get a quarterly statement informing me how much of commission I have earned in the last quarter from active policies I sold in early 2000.

Siddharth cleared the 12th standard in 2003 and turned 18 that year. He wanted to start working and asked me for help with his resume. He cleared the very first interview he went for and joined one of the better ITES companies in Pune. He came back very excited from his first day of work and informed me that there were people my age working alongside him in his process.

So, I pulled out the addresses of the ITES companies and started visiting them. Companies were conducting walk-in interviews and anyone could walk in with their CVs and get interviewed. At every place, I was politely informed that I did not meet their requirement. Not because I was 46 years of age but because I had done nothing in the past that they could consider as experience other than selling. That too in the early 1980s.

At one place I met an extremely involved recruiter, who pulled out a form, wrote down my personal details, and then proceeded to make a note of all I had done in my 25 years of working life. He then systematically scored me item by item on his list and wrote a '0' in each column. At the end of his labour, he informed me with pride that based on his organization's criteria my potential for selection in an ITES company was a big fat ZERO.

Around this time a very stylish couple moved into one of the row houses and the society was buzzing with titbits of information about them. They were not only young, good-looking, drove a fancy car but also owned a dog that looked like a lion. I was introduced to the couple through someone who had gotten introduced to them through another someone and before we knew it, we were all invited to their place for dinner. That evening we learned that the gentleman was working as the Manager Training at an ITES company close to our place. During the evening I let the host know that I was between assignments and was open to any opportunities. However, nothing came out of it.

The first weekend of May 2004, Siddharth and I decided to trek to Raj Machi, a place beyond Lonavala. Sid used to work the night shift and got back early on 1st May. We were packed and ready and left the moment he reached home. For two days we did not see a soul, we slept at the Raj Machi fort, cooked on wood collected from the hills, drank around the fire, and talked. We were trekking together after a long time because of his work and thoroughly enjoyed the experience.

The moment I reached home Pat informed me that the Training Manager had visited her twice on Saturday and four times on Sunday asking for me. She had also caught him on a few occasions swinging on our gate while expectantly looking at the main entrance of the township. She was sure that the squeaking from the gate had become worse over the last couple of days! As I had not observed this behaviour in him earlier, I knew it must be something important. I called him the moment I had showered and he was knocking on our door even before the call ended. I am sure he had been swinging on our gate again!

The gentleman walked in and said the following three sentences that changed my life and made it even remotely possible for me to write a book on human potential.

He said:

You are hired as a trainer

Report for work at 9:00 am tomorrow

The dress code is formal.

He left as swiftly as he had come, even before I could ask him any questions about the job. It appeared to me that he was trying to avoid any queries that I may have about my role. I honestly did not care as I was back in the corporate world and it also proved to me that my potential for landing a job in the ITES industry was more than ZERO.

I made plenty of calls that evening trying to find someone who could guide me as to what a trainer is supposed to do. Not a single person I contacted had ever trained or taught. Only one of the persons I knew had attended a training session and gave me a valuable piece of advice. She suggested that I keep asking the participants "Any Questions" at regular intervals to encourage "engagement". With this precious piece of information, I plunged into my new career.

I reported for work as instructed and in the course of being introduced to the rest of the team, I learned the reason for my unusual hiring experience. I believe the Manager Training had paid a surprise visit to one of the training sessions and had found the trainer leaning against the desk while doing her job. He had threatened to break her legs if he ever caught her doing it again. The lady was so upset she grabbed her bag and left. This happened on a Friday evening. Five new batches were starting on Monday and there were only four trainers. The existing trainers were so disgusted with the manager's style of functioning that they decided not to help. They wanted to watch the fun on Monday when the manager would be one trainer short. Instead, they found me.

For the manager training, it appears, the most important competency for a trainer was the ability to stand for eight hours without sitting or taking the support of any prop. He had noticed this capability in me when I had stood erect for six hours at his party while polishing off half a bottle of premium whiskey, without even once getting an urge to sit down or lean against the wall for support. I was ideal trainer material as far as my manager was concerned.

The training material was handed over to me and I was shown the room where 20 young souls were waiting for me to enlighten them on what would make them successful in their chosen profession. After a round of introductions, I started with the training. I would read one para from the course material, look into space and nod my head if the meaning was clear to me or shake it sideways if I wasn't too sure, then move on to the next para. However, in between each of these pauses, I would make it a point to ask "Any Questions?" and fortunately, there were none.

As most of the participants were right out of college, they were most probably used to this style of a teaching and found nothing unusual about my behaviour. On a couple of occasions that I did look at the participants, I noticed a blank look on most faces. That evening, I made it a point to read the next day's material thoroughly, make notes, and write down the questions that I could ask and examples I could share. The effectiveness of training and the engagement from participants improved gradually. Over the weekend I prepared like I was appearing for a Board exam and I was ready to take on the class.

I was very well prepared for the session on Monday, and that day something magical happened. The participants started proactively asking questions, sharing experiences, and challenging concepts. And I started enjoying what I was doing. 10th May 2004 was the second most important day of my life, the most important being my day of birth. On the 10th I discovered my purpose in life. Though it was not well articulated at this point in time, I knew that I wanted to help people in performing better and achieving more in life.

Over a period of time I have got absolute clarity about my purpose in life. Today, when I run my own consulting company, no mail introducing our company is ever sent out without the line *"TalentEdge was formed with the purpose of helping organizations and people tap into their potential."*

The batch passed out with flying colours and every 15 days we had a new set of people to train as the demand on the floor was never-ending. I started enjoying what I was doing and it also seemed to rub off on the trainees.

Within three months I got an offer to join a better organization as a Senior Trainer on a much better salary.

In December 2004, our daughter Gazal passed away under very tragic circumstances. Each one in the family chose their own means to tackle the loss. While I immersed myself completely in work, Pat chose religion and spirituality, Siddharth created an opaque shell around himself. All of us, however, were scarred for life. Some years later Siddharth moved to Australia for higher studies and is today an Australian national along with his wife Puja from Pune.

With Gazal watching over us, things moved very fast. My tenure at various levels in the different organizations that I worked was as follows:

Trainer - 3 months

Sr. Trainer - 9 months, where I migrated a process from the USA

AM Training - 12 months setting up the same process in Bangalore

Manager Training - 14 months in Pune with a different company

Geography Head - 18 months for a Chennai Based company working out of Pune, where I was introduced to Behavioural Training for the first time

AVP West - 16 months for NCR based Training Company working out of Mumbai

Sr. VP India and South Asia - 12 months working out of Bangalore for an NCR headquartered organization, selling signature training programs

VP Consulting - 24 months working out of Gurgaon for an NCR based Global HR Consulting company

In my last four roles, I was told that never in the history of the organization had they hired someone at this senior a position who was "just a graduate". They issued me the Appointment Letter all the same.

I have worked with many people during my professional journey and someone reading this book might say "What about Levo Consulting? I wonder why Rakesh hasn't mentioned that". Yes, I did start a training company with a very dear friend of mine. Our timing was totally off. One month after we launched our company there was a global financial meltdown in 2008. Training and L&D became the two most dispensable overheads for most organizations. Three months later I was back in the corporate world working out of Mumbai.

Another person may wonder why I have not mentioned my involvement with Multi-Level Marketing companies. Yes, I used to make the sales pitch for a few MLMs on weekends. It used to give me a high addressing an auditorium full of members and their prospective downlines and it was a great source of income during my school bus days.

God was kind to me as my journey from a Trainer to VP Consulting for a Global HR consulting company took just seven and a half years. From May 2014, I have been running my own HR consulting company quite successfully and have launched another one during the COVID-19 pandemic.

I hope God has also been kind to the person who had scored me ZERO on my potential to get hired. I pray to God he has a team to manage, and he is no longer scoring people himself. Instead, he is now collating and analysing the scores given by his team members.

The reason why I wanted to share my professional journey with the reader is twofold.

The first is to establish that I have enough exposure both as an employee and as an entrepreneur to be writing a book about "Leadership Potential". I have fortunately been employed by some of the best companies in the business and have got relevant exposure.

I have also run my own business for more than half of my working life, and most of my experience in L&D and Consulting has been as an external consultant with new and different clients each day. I have had exposure to the challenges faced by Fortune 500 companies and even those faced by promoter-driven companies with a turnover of a few crores. Each of these engagements is a learning experience and gives me insights into the similarities and diversity of challenges faced by them and the unique ways in which they address these challenges.

Second, to showcase how the corporate world defines relevant experience. The roles that gave me the greatest learnings, like the Army or running my Air Curtain business are not even considered as experience by the HR teams conducting the interview.

My experience in the L&D space as a consultant with scores of different companies from diverse industries allows for cross-pollination of ideas. Most companies, however, when approached for business still want to know how many of their competitors have I worked with. That becomes the criteria for selection. I try to reason that if I have already worked in your industry the solution that I will offer will most probably be from our repository. If I haven't, it will be through our research.

Another question that we hear often when we solicit business is "What do you know about our business?" and our response is that you are fortunate that I know nothing about your business. Hence the solutions we offer will most probably be unique and not an incremental improvement on what you or the industry is already doing.

This type of thinking is a throwback to the situation we had faced when I started my air curtain business. The question invariably asked was "Where else have you installed your Air Curtains." The quality of the equipment that I was demonstrating was less important to the buyer than the number of his competitors using our equipment.

The corporate world looks down on anyone who seeks a job after having run their own business. Their need to get back to a job paints them as a failure in the eyes of the recruiter. Instead of trying to leverage the learnings of the entrepreneur most companies disregard their experience, forcing one to start at the lowest level every time. Both the person and the organization suffer from this type of thinking.

In my role, we deal with very senior people in the organizations we serve. I have noticed in most cases the leaders have reached their current seniority while working only in one industry and on many occasions in the same department. This gives them a myopic view of the business reality and they are seldom open to creative solutions

I request you read this book with an open mind. It is absolutely fine to disagree with any thought process or challenge any concepts discussed here. My objective is to make leaders think and not for them to accept everything written here as the Gospel truth.

So, with not such a brief preface let us dive into what really constitutes Leadership Potential.

Chapter 1

Components of Potential

Leadership Potential is a term widely used in board rooms and the HR fraternity but its precise meaning is difficult to pin down. Though tapping into human potential is critical for the success of an organization, what constitutes "Leadership Potential", is often not clearly understood. It is often confused with other competencies and traits that may have made certain people successful professionally in the short to medium term, but may still not represent true Leadership Potential.

In the absence of an accurate definition of leadership potential and a lack of a clear understanding of what it means, it is quite possible organizations may be spending their finite resources of time and energy focusing on traits and competencies that have little or no relation to leadership potential. This is something no organization can afford in a world that is becoming more competitive and an environment where resources are scarce and their optimal deployment the difference between success and failure.

The feature that most distinguishes human beings from animals is higher-order consciousness or our ability to choose. This means that we have the potential to decide what we make of ourselves. In the corporate space, a majority of the people aspire to be great leaders – with only a handful choosing to be subject matter experts - however, most people are confused about what makes leaders great, people who are remembered and revered long after they have moved out of an organization or passed on from this world.

At the most, basic level Leadership Potential is the inherent ability that an employee must have to grow within the organization. Also, to help the organization grow and capture market share, create more satisfied customers, stay competitive in a business environment that is becoming more demanding and in a scenario, where no organization is considered too big to fail.

The potential of an employee is the ability to successfully take on more diverse responsibilities and/or to progress up the corporate ladder and effectively assume more authority and lead larger teams, own bigger stakes, and create a larger impact on the outcomes for the organization.

Potential is what organizations are looking out for while hiring laterally or promoting from within their ranks. However, what constitutes potential is not always clear leading to wrong hiring or promotions with disastrous consequences for the team and organization.

Often, performance is believed to represent potential. An above-average performer is believed to have the ability to lead effectively at the next level and therefore gets promoted. However, potential is something way beyond performance or the ability to deliver the numbers, even though potential cannot exist without consistent above-average performance being an important part of it.

Every business is in the business of making money and the only way to make money in a sustainable manner is to add value to customers on an ongoing basis. The moment an organization stops delivering something of value to clients it becomes irrelevant and falls by the wayside.

Even the best organizations get pushed aside by newcomers who better understand the current and future explicit and implicit needs of the customers and do something about addressing them. Corporate history is littered with carcasses of organizations that were once great but are struggling to survive today or no longer exist. The Fortune 500 list is a prime example of companies regularly being replaced by new ones every year.

Great leadership is essential for business success. It is one of the most important factors, if not the most important, for an organization's success as it transforms potential into reality. Leadership not only in the current role but the potential for future leadership is what organizations need to invest in, as every organization plans to grow and create customer loyalty in various ways.

The Peter Principle correctly observes that people get promoted to their level of incompetence i.e. employees are promoted based on their success in the previous role until they reach a level at which they are no longer competent, as skills at one level do not necessarily translate into the skill requirement of the next level.

According to the Peter Principle, over a period of time all crucial positions in an organization are held by individuals who are struggling with living up to the expectations of the role. The challenge for most organizations today is to find leaders who don't reach their level of incompetence in the near future and have the capacity to reinvent themselves on an ongoing basis to meet the new set of expectations at each level.

The general belief is that companies compete based on their products and/or services, though the reality is that they compete on the basis of the potential of their leaders. Better leaders create more engaged and empowered employees, who in turn create better products and services to satisfy the needs of their customers, giving the company a competitive edge.

The success of a company will, to a very large extent depend on its ability to create more effective leaders with greater potential, faster than the competition. Very few companies however give the development of human capital the importance it deserves.

Today we have entered the Human age (a term coined by the Manpower group) having passed through the stone age, metal age, agriculture age, industrial age, space-age, knowledge worker age, to name a few. In the Human Age, it is believed that the most important differentiator for an organization is the quality of people that the organization possesses. People are no longer looked upon as a resource that is replaceable but as talent that is unique and capable of contributing towards the organization's success in its own distinctive manner.

Success, or lack of it for an organization, in the Human Age, will therefore depend on, whether it can attract, develop and retain high potential individuals. Technology, location and product are no longer the differentiators in most cases but are an outcome of the talent available to the organization.

Most organizations accept that people are their biggest assets, however very few put their money where their mouth is. Organizations provide preventive maintenance to assets like machinery, vehicles and equipment and only breakdown maintenance to their leadership. They service and maintain machinery to ensure minimal unplanned downtime but provide training, coaching and mentoring support to employees only when there is a breakdown situation and the manager is struggling with the situation, causing major disruptions to operations and consequential revenue loss.

Organizations critically examine and scrutinise their financial balance sheet as it is an indicator of the health of the organization, however, only a handful of organizations give the same importance and focus to their talent balance sheet. They seem disinterested in ascertaining where talent resides within the organization and who are the people contributing to the outcomes that the organization desires to achieve in the long run. They don't seem to realize that in the medium to long term it is the health of their talent balance sheet that will influence the financial balance sheet of the organization.

HR in most organizations is busy rectifying shortcomings in people, instead of focusing on developing and tapping into the potential of employees. Organizations forget that if they want to create capital they have to invest in their people first.

I started my career as a salesperson 43 years back and have been selling ever since. In all the organizations but one, where I worked in a sales role, I was not provided any sales training beyond being taught about the technical details of the product and maybe some pointers about how to present the features to the prospect and a bit about body language if the manager was really engaged in developing her sales team. Most managers don't seem to realize that there is much more to selling than presenting the features of the product in an understandable manner.

Only one organization took us through a weeklong training workshop where they helped the future salespersons understand the different steps involved in the sales process and the importance of uncovering explicit and implicit needs of customers. The training also taught us the importance of building trust with the customer before closing a sale. We were trained to become trusted advisors to the customers and not just salesmen trying to meet our targets. Today we run a very popular program based on "High-Value Sales" and it has made a difference to the top line of many companies.

Most managers believe that selling is something that comes intuitively to people and does not need to be taught hence a sales person is sent out in the field with little or no knowledge about what constitutes selling, thereby setting them up for failure.

The same happens when a person moves into the role of a first-time manager from being an individual contributor. It is assumed that a person will seamlessly move into the mould of a manager. As a manager, for the first time in her career, her success is dependent on the success of the team. As an individual contributor, however, success was an outcome of her ability to deliver more than her peers individually, thereby achieving, and exceeding targets. It was all about how fast a person could learn the task and how much a person could deliver personally.

Most first-time managers continue to work as individual contributors even after being promoted to a managerial role, only working three times harder as they are now trying to meet their targets and those of their team members through a Herculean effort on their part. Delegating authority and responsibility, coaching and mentoring, handholding and supporting are traits that they may not have experienced themselves as individual contributors and may not be very comfortable deploying when it comes to their team members.

Support in the form of generic training will be provided to a first-time manager usually only when she is found to be struggling in her new role. This experience of damage control is repeated at every level in the organization where people are thrown into the deep end without support or a safety net. They are referred to HR for some performance improvement engagements only when found to be struggling to deliver the desired results. Just imagine the loss in productivity and results in an organization where most of the workforce is working at a fraction of their potential.

While organizations compete in the 21st century, the majority of them are still shaped, organizationally, by 20th-century management ideas. One leader who has managed to challenge this state of affairs is Vineet Nayar, Vice-chairman and CEO of HCL Technologies. He believes that most employees have more potential than the organization allows them to demonstrate. Vineet inverted the organizational pyramid, empowering employees to be change agents and created a culture of transparency and trust with very positive outcomes for his organization.

"Today's youth work very differently to anything we've seen before. They are natural collaborators, communicators, innovators. We just need to give them the tools they need, and get out of their way"

– Vineet Nayar

As organizations are unable to define leadership potential accurately, they do not know where to concentrate their people development efforts. One observes employees being subjected to sporadic training programs on very generic topics, mentoring programs that die out over a period of time and assessment centres which lead nowhere, being offered in most organizations. This is because organizations are not clear about where they need to focus their energies and invest their funds.

In this book, I will try to demystify "Leadership Potential". Leadership potential has within itself the scope for growth and achievement. Our potential is not there to stagnate but to grow and bring into existence the outcomes that we desire as we move forward in life. Hence a person or an organization should be able to understand the different components of Leadership Potential with enough clarity that they can take effective action to do something about developing them.

The principles we mention here will apply to our lives outside of work, as well as our professional careers. Most people spend a substantial part of their lives working while also trying to maintain a balance between work and their personal lives. The distinction between the two is blurring constantly in a world that is so connected especially now when work from home or work from anywhere has become the new normal.

The term work-life balance is normally used very loosely implying that work is outside of life. In fact, work is very much a part of life. Most people when using the term work-life balance imply that one must suffer work for at least 40 hours a week so that they can live life for the balance of the time. It however does not have to be so. If one is leveraging one's potential, in a work environment that is conducive to demonstrating your best results, then work can be as exciting and rewarding as anything else we do and Monday morning blues should be a thing of the past.

So let us take a closer look at components of "Leadership Potential". The 5th and the final "P" of Leadership is "Potential", the other four being Purpose, Performance, Perception and Personality.

One can claim to be living up to her potential only if the other 4 P are in place and are aligned to create the best impact. Misalignment in any of the four Ps or a lack of one or more will lead to a person's potential being compromised. Such an employee will not be firing on all cylinders but would be limping along on her corporate/life journey. Hence it becomes essential for us to have absolute clarity about the ingredients that constitute leadership potential in a manner that can lead to "actionables" which in turn should lead to the desired outcomes.

A Closer look at the 4Ps:

Purpose: People need to be clear about their purpose in life. They need an inner focus to be aware of their own feelings, values and intuitions and to manage themselves well. They need an internal compass that keeps them on track to the true north. Without a clear purpose in life, choices will be made based on convenience and not out of conviction and there will be very little motivation to excel. It is important to look around, have experiences and take stock and then define one's purpose with absolute clarity. One can only accomplish with excellence something one purposefully pursues.

Performance: Most organizations have robust processes in place to measure the performance of individuals and teams. Most performance management systems though, measure only a part of what constitutes true performance. Still, a disproportionate amount of energy and importance is normally given to performance and hence we have a Performance Management System (PMS) in place and regular performance reviews.

Performance, however, is the point of entry. One can't have potential unless one delivers superior performance on a regular basis. Performance, however, does not equal potential but is a small part of it. On many occasions organizations have confused performance with potential and have promoted people into leadership positions (to their level of incompetence) and ended up with leaders who are overwhelmed with the new reality, leading a bunch of people who are over managed, de-motivated and demoralized and performing way below their true potential.

Perception: One only has the potential to be a leader if people perceive one to be worth following. One can be a manager and lead a team of 15 people. One can even meet and exceed targets as a manager by mandating certain behaviours, actions and deliverables. This will still not make them a leader.

A leader is someone people choose to follow. While a manager has her designation and exercises authority to get the desired outcomes, a leader has moral authority over her team members and peers. People do the leaders' bidding because they want to and not because they have to. Management is related to designation whereas leadership can be displayed by anyone irrespective of their designation or years of work experience.

A leader is on stage all the time and being observed by team members, peers, seniors, stakeholders, etc. People form perceptions about them at every touch point. Perceptions get created either by default or design. It makes more sense to manage this important process as the right image is a very crucial part of leadership potential.

Personality: The dictionary definition of personality is "the combination of characteristics or qualities that form an individual's distinctive character." Leaders and people with leadership potential also possess and display certain personality traits that make them leaders.

The earlier view was that certain people are born leaders. Either you had it in you at birth, to be a leader or there was no scope for one to become a leader at any stage in life. Recent studies have shown that leadership is more competency and behaviour driven. If you display certain behaviours most people will perceive you to be a leader and hopefully follow you.

Potential: A person can be said to have the potential for leadership if the first four P's are aligned and working to the advantage of the leader. She has to be clear about her purpose in life, things that excite her and what does she want her contribution to be remembered as. She must be an above-average performer, giving superior results consistently, people should perceive her to be someone worth being led by and she should display the personality traits that a leader must have to succeed in today's competitive corporate world.

There is an acute shortage of leaders with the potential to lead effectively, who can grow with the role and contribute to the organization's growth over the medium and long term. People with leadership potential are not only in short supply within organizations but there is a dearth of real talent even in the market.

Attracting talent laterally is not only more expensive but also riskier as the current interviewing process is not very effective in differentiating between great talent and "great interviewees". The other challenge is that education, experience and the brands a person has worked for in the past do not seem to have a direct relationship to performance, still, many interviewers give these attributes undue importance ending up with over qualified and expensive employees who do not deliver great results. In such a scenario creating leadership potential within the organization becomes the most important task for leaders.

In this book, we will look at each of the components of leadership potential in more detail so one can have absolute clarity about what one can do to enhance personal leadership potential and for organizations to identify prospective leaders and handhold them through their journey to greatness.

Any individual wanting to excel in the corporate world can also utilize this information and tips provided in this book, enabling her to invest time and energy in acquiring those attributes that would increase her leadership potential. Organizations should shift their approach from breakdown maintenance to preventive maintenance when dealing with the most important asset of any organization. Identifying genuine high potentials and providing them with opportunities to hone their leadership skills would differentiate successful companies from those that failed.

Let us take a more detailed look at the four Ps that constitute potential to understand what they stand for and how we can make them work to our advantage.

Chapter 2

Purpose

The Purpose of Life is a Life of Purpose

– Robert Byrne

Purpose is a mental paradigm that acts as an inspiration for giving shape and direction to human thought and action. Having a well-defined purpose in life has long been recognized as an important component in enabling humans to tap into their true potential and to live a life of greater satisfaction and accomplishment. Knowing your life's purpose can give direction to your life and help you figure out where to focus your energy, time and resources.

When was the last time you asked yourself these important questions?

- What are my goals in life and what am I doing to achieve them?
- How valuable is my life and do I add value to someone else's life?
- Does my life matter to me and others?
- What will people remember me for after I die?

Honest answers to these questions will help you define your purpose in life.

It is truly one of man's greatest blessings to have the capability to choose their purpose in life, rather than live the life that other animals lead where their responses, desires and motivations are pre-programmed. It is indeed a double-edged sword, with one side having the potential to unlock within a person, powers that she had never dreamed she possessed and on the other, the potential to waste those exact powers by either not using or underutilizing them.

Purpose drives potential. The purpose of a seed is to unleash its potential. Inside a small seed resides the potential of the mighty oak tree or a tiny rose plant. Their purpose however is pre-decided and not an outcome of choices the seed makes. An oak seed will either not take root at all or will produce an oak tree each time. Whether it is a sickly oak tree or a mighty one will depend on the circumstances in which it existed and survived.

A rose plant seed will not produce an oak tree despite its greatest efforts. It will, by default grow into a rose plant every time as it is pre-programmed for that. The health and productivity of the rose tree will to a large extent depend on the nurturing it received.

Our role, as individuals, is far more complex and challenging. Where all those other forms of life do not have choices, we do. Those other forms of life are limited by and succeed through the natural laws; over which they have no control, to grow to their greatest possible potential. Hence an oak seed will, given the right circumstances produce an oak tree and likewise for a rose plant. In the case of humans, we can choose to be either a mighty oak or prickly rose bush and succeed in whatever we choose to be. Purpose creates this potential in humans, hence it is the foundation of our growth and development.

Lack of a clear purpose in life leads to a lot of activity with very little progress along desired lines. When a person does not know her destination every road looks promising. If all paths seem equally promising, being humans, we are likely to choose the easiest path to travel. However, it is usually not the easiest path that leads to greatness. Most great people have created their own path to success and that was possible as they were very certain about their life's purpose.

During my interactions with very senior leaders in the corporate world, I am surprised when people are unable to share their leadership purpose. Despite being in leadership positions for relatively long periods they don't have an immediate answer. They also struggle for an answer when asked, why they come to work each day. This is a clear indication that enough thought has not been given to the most important aspect of their leadership vision. The purpose is not articulated clearly enough to drive them to unleash their true potential. Under these circumstances how does one decide where to focus one's energy and time in one's corporate/ life journey?

The reason why most people do not have clarity about their purpose is not hard to find. As children, our purpose is usually dictated to us. Getting good grades seems to be the all-consuming purpose during our schooling days, with a little entertainment (secondary purpose) allowed on weekends. The second goal is usually sacrificed for attaining the first one where all pleasurable activities are subverted to studies when exams are around the corner.

Upon graduation, this purpose expires and a void is felt till it is replaced by the next purpose of higher studies or getting a cushy job. Even here for most people, the purpose is decided by others, who in this case may be parents, a consultant, or an expert in some field. They supposedly "help" students define their own purpose and guide them on the appropriate path.

What we take as our purpose is usually someone else's purpose that we have accepted as our own as we did not create one for ourselves. This is the main reason why we see so many people burning out at a young age along with associated physical and mental ailments. They are trying to be happy and successful while living someone else's dreams.

Some people however break away from convention and choose to create their own path or tread the same path that others have tread before them, but in their own fashion. What guides them through this journey is a clear articulation of their purpose. The purpose is something that becomes a beacon for them to drive them to fulfillment and success. This purpose is a combination of their values, convictions and life goals. These are also the people who excel in their chosen field and lead fulfilling lives.

You may have observed that success is not natural and does not come to everyone. In every field, only a handful of people succeed. Coincidentally they are also the very same people who have a very strong purpose and have absolute clarity about what they want their lives to look like. In their minds, they have already defined their success criteria and a game plan for being successful. As they have a strong purpose they do not get easily distracted and focus all their energies on trying to achieve what is important for them.

Purpose defines the destination and allows one to plan the journey.

A sailor navigating the high seas in a sailboat normally knows the destination the boat is heading for. Their goal or purpose is well defined. It is however very unlikely that one will get favourable winds right through the journey. On occasions the wind will be nudging the boat towards the destination, helping in the accomplishment of the goal and at other times the winds will push the boat away from the destination. The sailor overcomes the challenge of adverse winds by adjusting the sails to head in the general direction of her destination. The path may not always be straight and would most probably zig zag across the ocean. If the destination is clear the boat will eventually reach it.

In the absence of a clear destination, the sailor would let the winds decide the course of the journey and the fate of the boat. The place where the boat finally touches land will be decided by the direction of the winds and not by some internal compass. Most of us lead our lives in a similar manner in the absence of a well-defined purpose. Several of us lead lives where events and people decide our destination for us. We end up living a life of convenience rather than a life of conviction. Hence, we see the lack of drive and initiative in most people, in trying to achieve excellence in life.

A strong purpose in life has other benefits too beyond providing us with direction and identifying areas where we should be expending our time and energy. Let us look at some other payoffs of a clear purpose in life.

Health:

Since childhood, we have been taught that health is wealth. There is enough material available on the net and elsewhere about what constitutes a healthy lifestyle. The focus usually is on healthier eating habits, more activity and getting sufficient rest being made part of our lifestyles. These may be important for being healthy but not sufficient as without a strong purpose ill health may still follow one through life.

In a study conducted in Japan where over 73000 people were monitored, showed that people who had a stronger sense of purpose (which is called ikigai in Japanese) tended to live longer than people who did not have a definite purpose. A 2014 research in Japan showed that having a strong purpose acted as a barrier against mortality risk in old age. Dan Buettner in his research identified the factors that most centenarians share. One common factor across all centenarians was a strong purpose.

Another study in 2008 showed an inverse relationship between life purpose and cardiovascular disease. More research in this area showed that "purpose is a possible protective factor against near-future myocardial infarction among those with coronary heart disease."

In studies of thousands of elderly subjects, Dr. Patricia Boyle, a neuropsychologist at the Rush Alzheimer's Disease Center in Chicago, found that people with a low sense of life purpose were 2.4 times more likely to get Alzheimer's disease than those with a strong purpose. Further, people with a well-articulated purpose in life were less likely to develop impairments in daily living and mobility disabilities.

Further research by Dan Buettner, identified that the two most vulnerable times in a person's life are the first twelve months after birth and the first year after retirement. You most probably personally know perfectly healthy people whose' health started deteriorating shortly after they retired from a lifelong career or profession. Some researchers suspect that for these people, the end of their career also signified the end of their purpose in life, which in turn affected their health and wellbeing.

We commit ourselves to get healthier at regular intervals. Most new year resolutions are about getting fitter by drinking less, eating intelligently, exercising more, and getting sufficient rest. The resolutions are made with all seriousness and commitment. However, they normally don't last long. Very soon we are back to our old lifestyle but sincerely make the same resolution the very next year to be broken again in all probability. There may be a better way of staying healthy and active as there is direct and irrefutable evidence that people with a strong purpose lead healthier and more fulfilling lives. Their purpose drives their behaviours and actions.

On the other hand, we frequently see young, supposedly healthy people take critically ill and even die suddenly of a heart attack or some other lifestyle disease. These are people who often frequent gyms, participate in marathons and are normally conscious about their diet. Even after these precautions they still fall critically ill rather early in life. These could be cases of people working very hard at jobs that are not aligned to their purpose in life or their professional purpose. They could be slogging away at someone else's purpose which they have accepted as their own without really buying into it.

A study conducted at Shell showed that people who chose to retire at 55 as against the permissible retirement age of 65 in their organization, were more likely to die at an earlier age. A study conducted over 17000 persons in Greece shows that the chances of death soon after retirement rose by 51percent. This could be attributed to people not having a personal purpose in life and experiencing a void once their professional purpose was exhausted.

These two studies suggest that there may be some risk in only finding meaning in a career. It seems important to restructure life's big questions and find ways to continue having a strong purpose even after retirement to improve the chances of a longer, healthier, and meaningful life.

It has long been part of physicians' legend that people with a positive, purpose-driven outlook on life are relatively resistant to disease as well as hardships in general. Neurologist and psychiatrist Viktor Frank, who was held in German concentration camps during World War II, observed: "that those with a sense of meaning in life were better able to cope with the horrific circumstances in the concentration camps,".

The three greatest days of your life are the day you were born, the day you find out what your purpose is in life and the day you die, but if you don't know what your purpose is then you don't know why you are here, and it can be hard to keep going on with enthusiasm and passion when not driven by an all-consuming purpose.

The most important benefit of creating a strong professional and personal purpose is that it allows us to create our own personal and professional brand. Normally these two should be aligned and complement one another. Not many people give enough thought to the brand or legacy they will be leaving behind as they do not see the value of thinking about or beyond death. They consequently do not invest enough time and energy in defining their personal and professional brand. Unfortunately, today people are more conscious about the brands they consume than the brand they themselves are.

There are two types of people in this world. One spread happiness wherever they go and the second whenever they go. Are we even aware of which category we currently belong to? Have we given this question serious thought? We can however choose to spread happiness by our presence and our life purpose will help us get there.

Let us look at the history and significance of brands. Branding of cattle started around 1650 to establish ownership, later brands were burned onto wooden cases to guarantee good quality wine. Gradually more and more products and services started getting branded and brands are very big business today.

Today almost anything can be branded so there exist very recognizable products, services, people and places as brands. Your brand has arrived if it is used as a verb, hence we have people asking us to Xerox documents, Hoover the carpet, Photoshop a picture, Skype the family and Google information.

But brands also work differently. Now individuals are seen as their own brand. Your brand is what people will remember you as, much after you have left the organization or passed on from this world. Your Brand is the values, abilities and experiences that people associate with you. The challenge with your personal or professional brand is that it can either be created by design, where you stay in control of it, or by default, where it just happens. In the absence of a clear and well-defined purpose, it is not possible to create your own personal and professional brand by design.

Let us try to understand the importance of our personal brand or the legacy that we will be leaving behind. From the moment one is born, life is in a race with death. This is one race that death never loses. The certainty of death is known to each one of us but for some strange reason, we don't like to think about it. We seldom, if ever visualize ourselves dead, being carried to our final resting place, depending on the religion we follow, by our friends and family. Though we constantly fret about minor issues that may or may not even take place, we avoid thinking about the most catastrophic challenge that we will ever face in our lives.

Once one is dead and gone, few people will discuss the size of the house one lived in or the car one drove or even the last designation one held. The discussions will be about what one did for others, the experiences that one gave others and how one made them feel. In the absence of a clear purpose in life, how will one decide what experiences one wants to give others and what one wants to be remembered as?

Our brand is the only thing that we will own even after death, whereas all our worldly possessions will belong to others. We normally give undue importance to the assets that we accumulate in our life without realizing that we don't own them. You don't own the house by the sea that you had saved for half your life. Once you are dead and gone, the house will still be there but someone else will be calling it "my house". You don't own the house; the house owns you.

The same will be the case with the other assets we have worked so hard to acquire. The only thing that will still be ours post our demise, is the personal brand we have created, that no one can take away from us. One has between today and the day one dies – which could be any day – to create the brand that will outlive us. It is impossible to create a personal and professional brand in the absence of clarity of purpose.

One can hence conclude that creating a strong purpose professionally and in our personal lives is an investment worth making as the rewards outstrip the efforts manifold.

I conduct an ice-breaking activity in my workshops where I ask people to share three "facts" about themselves. Two facts are true while the third one is a blatant lie, but presented as a fact. The rest of the participants are expected to guess which "fact" is a lie. This is an activity where people have fun, the ice is broken and people find so many new things about the other participants.

One thing I invariable notice is that most people talk about things that they used to do when they were younger. All their pleasant memories and accomplishments seem to be from the past. When I ask them if they enjoyed doing those activities, the answer is invariably a resounding YES. When I probe further as to why they don't do those pleasurable activities anymore the standard answer is that now they are working, and they do not have the time.

People are so busy living someone else's purpose, that they have stopped doing stuff that is important and enjoyable for them. Isn't this an ideal recipe for immense inner turmoil and a feeling of being overwhelmed, disconnected and frustrated?

Zig Ziglar has put this sentiment rather well when he observes "You need a plan to build a house. To build a life, it is even more important to have a plan or goal." Unfortunately, most of us are so busy driving that we don't have time to fill gas. How can we expect positive outcomes from life if this is our thought process?

Let us recognize the reasons why so few people have identified their purpose in life. Let us figure out why so many of us go through life like a sailboat that has a sail but no one to set the sail and where the direction of the winds has the most influence on our journey through life. There seem to be two reasons why most people do not have a clearly articulated personal and professional purpose and a well-defined action plan for achieving or purpose in life.

It appears that most of us have not understood the importance of articulating our purpose so we haven't devoted any time or energy to this activity. We are so busy with mundane activities that we don't have time for the important things in life. The other reason could be the fear of failure. When you don't have a clearly defined purpose that you need to accomplish, then any achievement can be treated as a success. One does not have to take charge of one's life and circumstances and events outside our control can be blamed for everything. The point to be noted is that successful people also face challenges but still come out triumphant as their purpose drives them through challenging times.

Finding your professional and personal purpose is not as difficult or complex as it may appear, however before a person can get to formalizing one's purpose it is important to have as many experiences as possible.

Most of us live lives where we like to do things that we are comfortable with or know how to do well, shunning new activities and experiences as they can lead to failure. Our risk aversion ensures that we work and live within a narrow band which is not a reflection of our true capabilities. This band is what is normally referred to as "Our Comfort Zone". What we tend to forget is that life begins outside our comfort zone, within the comfort zone it is only existence.

If one wants to identify a purpose that can serve one for a lifetime, then one will have to broaden one's horizons with experiences that one has not had so far. This can apply at the personal level as we try out different activities and experiences and professionally where we take on different responsibilities and roles.

I found my purpose at the age of 46 and that too accidentally. At that time, I was not aware of the importance of purpose. My career graph changed completely once I had a clearly defined professional purpose, as I could give it my undivided attention and energy.

Identifying one's purpose is not a left-brain activity. It needs both sides of the brain to work and the heart also has a major role to play in this activity. Ask yourself what is it that you love? Start taking steps to do what you enjoy doing. When you are motivated and connected to your inner self, inspiration floods your heart and soul. When you lead from your heart, you are happier, imaginative and driven to explore and experiment with new things and venture into the unknown. By doing what you love, you will be inspired and gain insights into what brings you the most happiness.

In short identify those activities and experiences, personal and professional, that make your heart sing. These are times when you feel really alive, have unlimited energy, no problem seems unbeatable, you are enjoying what you do and easily manage to find the time for these activities even in the most chaotic schedule.

Many of us struggle because we try to find that ONE thing that we want to accomplish; but trying to find only one thing is the reason why we feel like something is missing. The notion that we have only one thing we are meant for limits us from fulfilling our greatness. One has to look at the different roles one plays as a professional and also in one's private life. Shortlist the ones you are most passionate about and enjoy. Identify the behaviours associated with success in those roles and give them disproportionate energy and focus. When you live a life of passion you are living your life on purpose.

If you don't live your days by personal goals and plans, chances are you spend most of your time caught up in a flurry of day-to-day activities which don't serve any meaningful purpose for you. Do you ever get the feeling that your days are passing you by without any tangible outcomes to account for the efforts?

If you take a closer look at the things you have done in the recent past and the things you're planning to do next – Do, they mean anything to you if you are to die today? If not, then either you do not have a clearly defined purpose or you are not striving to achieve your purpose. One must plan ahead for all the high points you want in your life.

It is a brilliant idea to create a bucket list with timelines by which the tasks on your bucket list will be achieved. It is an incredibly insightful exercise as it not only highlights things that are important for you but also your commitment level towards achieving these goals.

The whole point of creating our bucket list is to be engaged in every moment of our existence and have a meaningful life. It's a reminder of all the things we want to achieve during our time here so that instead of wasting our time in pointless activities, we are directing our energy and efforts completely toward what really matters to us.

The questions that you may want to ask yourself are:

- What would you do if you had unlimited time, money and energy?
- How many of the items from your bucket list have been ticked off?
- What are your biggest goals and dreams?
- What are the important items you want to achieve on priority?
- What proficiencies/skills/competencies do you want to master?
- Are there any special moments you want to experience?
- What do you need to do to lead a life of the greatest meaning for you?

Come up with as many items as you can. Then create an action plan for achieving every item on your list.

A simple and effective way of identifying your purpose in life is to imagine that it is your 60th birthday and your last day at work. It is your send-off party and your boss, peers, reports and stakeholders have all gathered together for your send-off. Each group is going to raise a toast for you. You need to decide what are the two sentences or adjectives that you would like to hear from each group, describing you, when they raise a toast. Please make sure to capture not what they are most likely to say about you today, but what you would like to hear from each one of them when they speak about their association with you.

We have done this exercise often in our workshops and have noticed that all people want to hear positive traits that describe them, however, each person's list is different from others in some unique ways. So while one person would like to be remembered by her boss for her quality of work for the other person it was important to be known as someone who went after audacious targets with energy and enthusiasm. For some being available to team members was important while for others being remembered as a coach mattered more. Everyone's list is unique based on their priorities, which in turn defined their purpose.

Lock yourself in a quiet place and do this exercise seriously as it will give you valuable insight about what is important for you as your legacy. You may realize what is being said currently about you is different from your expectations. With your focus to deliver the numbers, you may not have been giving enough importance to how you are going about achieving the targets. Or that in your effort to provide the best to the family you may be neglecting the family itself. This approach towards life is bound to have unpleasant consequences.

The statements that you desire to hear, should normally also enable you to create an action plan to achieve the desired result. To be remembered as an empowering boss who enabled the team members to explore their potential, starting today you will have to become less risk-averse, have more faith in your team members, delegate more of your work to others and mentor and coach them to success. Only then can you make it part of your legacy.

To be remembered by your boss as responsible and trustworthy puts a huge amount of positive pressure on you to ensure that every time you deliver work to your manager it has to be of excellent quality and delivered on time. It may also involve keeping yourself updated about the latest in your domain as your manager may not trust your competency if you are not abreast with the latest developments in your field. It would also mean leading a life of integrity where you always do what you say and red flag scenarios early on, where you may not be able to live up to your word.

It is recommended to repeat the activity by imagining that your family and friends are raising the toast for you. If you want to be remembered as an awesome mom/dad, you will first and foremost have to find time for your kids in your busy work schedule, understand them, stand by them even when they make serious mistakes, be less judgemental and more supportive in their journey to adulthood.

When I did this activity for the first time it was an eye-opener for me. It gave me a lot of insight as to how I had to mend my behaviour and priorities if I wanted to have a chance in hell to hear the things that I was hoping to hear from my colleagues and family.

During that activity, I realized that I wanted to hear from my son that I was a great dad who was more like a friend and was always available when he needed me. When I analysed my work schedule I realised that in my pursuit of a bigger paycheque and faster promotions I had been focusing all my energies towards work at the cost of spending quality time with the family. Unfortunately, by the time the realization dawned on me he was already a teenager with his own friends and set of priorities. I however made a conscious effort to engage with him as often as possible and today we are much closer than we have ever been. Even though he has migrated to another country we are closer today than when we lived under the same roof and I am confident that today he looks upon me as his friend and a good dad.

The effectiveness of this exercise depends entirely on the seriousness and sincerity with which you conduct it. Once you have your answers you would normally be able to create an action plan to achieve the desired outcomes. We only have time between now and the day we die to create this legacy. This legacy is also the only thing that we will own after we are dead and gone. Though we know the day we were born, unfortunately, we don't know the day we will die. Let us show a sense of urgency by believing that today could be the last day to work towards creating our desired brand.

Purpose is the foundation around which we can plan to build our professional careers and personal lives. If we do not invest enough time and energy in identifying our purpose, we may wander through life without achieving much and being unhappy and overwhelmed through the journey.

Most of us lead truncated lives as we do not have a purpose strong and large enough to push us towards our true potential. As we think small, seldom venturing out of our comfort zone we also lead lives that are mediocre by most standards.

Let us do a simple mental exercise. Let us assume that you have been convicted for a crime that you either did or did not commit and the sentence for the crime is life imprisonment. Life in this case is not a 14 years sentence but a sentence for life where you will not be released from prison till the day you die.

I am sure it is going to be a shattering piece of news but there is a ray of hope. The Judge allows you to choose the cell in which you want to spend the rest of your life. The options for the size of the cell are 6X6ft, 10X10ft, or a cell that is 40X40ft in size. As we are going to spend the rest of our life locked up in this cell, I am sure most of us will choose the largest possible cell that we are entitled to.

Surprisingly, most people do not use the same logic in real life. Most people create small mental cells that they spend the rest of their lives in. Every time you decide that you can't do something you bang an iron bar into the ground defining the size of your cell. Thoughts like, "I can't trust another person as my girlfriend/boyfriend ditched me in college", "I can't start a business as no one in my family has ever been in business" or "I should not start a business because my friend tried her hand at it and suffered heavy losses". "I should not be riding a bike as I am married and have the responsibilities of being there for my kids", "I will not start a new hobby as I may make a fool of myself" and so on. The size of our cell is defined by the things we tell ourselves that we can't do or should not do.

Unfortunately for most people, the definition of failure is incorrect, directly impacting our success rate. Most people associate failure with not being able to achieve set targets or goals or failing to master some skill. The real definition of failure is "not even trying". There is a Japanese adage that says "Fall down seven times, stand up eight" Failure is when you don't get up after you fall or when you don't even try to do something because a positive outcome is not guaranteed.

This is however not the case with people who live enriched and full lives driven by their purpose and their vision about what really matters to them. My role model in this space is Mark Inglis, a Mountaineer from New Zealand.

This is what Wikipedia has to say about him.

"Born in Geraldine,[1] Inglis began work as a professional mountaineer in 1979 as a search and rescue mountaineer for Aoraki / Mount Cook National Park. In 1982 Inglis and climbing partner Philip Doole were stuck in a snow cave on Aoraki / Mount Cook for 13 days due to an intense blizzard. The rescue of the two climbers was a major media event in New Zealand. Both men's legs became badly frostbitten while awaiting rescue. Following Inglis's rescue, both his legs were amputated 14 cm below the knee. He returned to Mt. Cook in 2002 and reached the summit successfully on 7 January of that year, after a previous attempt was thwarted by problems with his legs. The summit assault in January 2002 was documented by the film No Mean Feat: The Mark Inglis Story.

On 27 September 2004, he successfully climbed Cho Oyu with three others, becoming only the second double amputee to summit a mountain greater than 8,000 metres (26,000 ft) in height.

On 15 May 2006, after 40 days of climbing, Inglis became the first-ever double amputee to reach the summit of Mount Everest, the highest mountain in the world. While acclimatizing at 6,400 metres (21,000 ft), a fixed-line anchor failed, resulting in Inglis falling and breaking one of his carbon fiber prosthetic legs in half. It was temporarily repaired with duct tape, while a spare was brought up from base camp. Inglis's Everest expedition was filmed for the Discovery Channel series Everest: Beyond the Limit."

If you read his book "Legs on Everest" detailing his preparations for the summit assault you realize that he had made a commitment to himself to climb Mt. Everest when he was trapped at Mount Cook in an intense blizzard in 1982. This was even before he knew that he would be losing both his legs. His commitment to climb Mt. Everest was so strong that he did not let small issues like having no legs come in the way of accomplishing his dream.

It took Mark 20 years before he could climb Mount Cook again and another 4 years before he could summit Mount Everest. Just imaging the strength of his purpose that allowed him to stay focused on climbing and maintaining the fitness level necessary for this feat.

People like Mark have chosen a cell that has no iron bars and he is empowered to roam free and live life on his terms, not bound by conventional thinking or wisdom. On his return to New Zealand after climbing Mt. Everest, both his stumps had to be amputated again because of the severe damage they had suffered during the climb and he lost another 5 digits from his hands. This did not stop him from leading a full life where he could accomplish more than what most of us will ever dream to achieve. What works for Mark is that he has a very clear and strong purpose and was willing to back his purpose with meaningful action.

We all know of people with an equally strong purpose and outstanding achievements, from other fields too, who have accomplished great things against insurmountable odds. Why do we know about them? Because there are a handful of people who stand out from the crowd. These people are driven by a purpose that is so powerful that they can overcome anything that circumstances throw at them. We can also choose to be part of this league.

Chapter 3

Performance

The second P of Leadership Potential is Performance. Without delivering consistently above-average performance one cannot stake a claim to being a high potential. What constitutes high performance is debatable though as most organizations track the wrong parameters while assessing the performance of individual contributors, managers and leaders.

Most organizations have a Performance Management System that is designed to evaluate the contributions of an employee at regular intervals. The frequency could be monthly, half-yearly, yearly, or any other frequency that the organization chooses. The objective of this system is to assess an employee's work performance and measure their contribution towards the achievement of organizational goals. Like any system, the effectiveness of the performance management system depends on how scientifically the system has been designed and how the process is deployed.

Let us take a closer look at the reality of business to understand what true performance looks like. This is one place where I find a lack of clarity, even with the senior-most leaders in the organizations we work with.

I like to ask prospective and existing clients to describe their business in one line or sentence. The responses I generally get are in line with, "we are in the business of clean energy", "we are in the telecom business", "We are in the business of servicing clients", "we are in the steel business" etc. While these answers are partially correct they are incomplete and miss out on the sole reason for the business to exist.

The correct answers to the following three questions would give any person true insight into the real business they are in:

Q1) Which business is our organization in?

A1) Our organization is in the business of making money. Different companies have chosen different routes to make money like clean energy, telecom or steel, however, the sole purpose of any business is to make money.

Q2) Which is the best and most sustainable way of making money in the long run?

A2) We can only sustainably make money by creating an ever-increasing number of satisfied customers

Q3) Whose responsibility in the organization is it to create satisfied customers?

A3) It is every department's and every employee's responsibility to create satisfied customers.

These questions can be peeled further like an onion and will give you deeper insight into your business.

The next logical extension to question Q 1) would be "How can a business make money?

- By increasing the top line.

- By decreasing wastages and spillages.

I can see at least 10 projects that an organization can undertake to increase the top line and improve efficiencies.

Q2) How do we create satisfied customers.

- By understanding and addressing the stated and unstated needs of customers

- Designing systems and solutions that are effective from the lens of the customer and not something that is convenient for the organization.

There is plenty of scope for concrete action that can be taken to disrupt competition and provide the best possible service to customers.

Q3) If everyone and every department is responsible for creating satisfied customers what can be done.

- Employees need to understand the importance of inter-department collaboration and synergies.

- Educate even those departments that have no external facing clients about how they impact customer satisfaction.

If we have so much clarity about the business we are in, decision-making becomes much easier as noise and clutter are done away with. Very few leaders, however, look at their business from this lens. Most organizations believe they are in the business of providing some product or service that clients need and it is the responsibility of marketing and the customer care department to create satisfied customers. Nothing could be further from the truth.

Most leaders heading departments that have little or no external interactions genuinely feel that they are in no way responsible for ensuring customer satisfaction. If finance delays the payment to a vendor, leading to delayed supplies, would the delay not lead to a chain reaction leading to eventually creating dissatisfied customers. Similarly, if compliance or procurement delays the execution of a contract, would it not lead to hindered completion of a project and consequently dissatisfied customers. I have met people from certain departments in many companies, who claim that their responsibility is to hold up files. According to them, it demonstrates that they are doing their job honestly.

Considering the above understanding of business, performance is much more than just achieving monthly and yearly targets. In the Performance Management System, more emphasis should be given to how the targets are achieved, rather than just on the achievement of targets. However, most performance management systems focus only on the achievement of targets as an indication of high performance. To complicate the situation further, most organizations end up confusing high performers with high potential as at some point the distinction between performance and potential blurs so much that the terms are generally used interchangeably.

There are three pillars of performance that any individual in the organisation focuses one's time and energy on. They are Strategy, Execution and People or Talent Management.

How many performance management systems track the strategic mind-set of a leader or the time, effort and resources spent by a leader on developing talent? Most don't and that is what makes the system ineffective, leading to people with potential being marked lower than target achievers.

Let us take a closer look at the three pillars to clearly understand their importance and significance in the success of an organization.

Strategy:

*"Creating value for humanity should not be an afterthought
but a core business strategy."*

– Anonymous

The English dictionary states that strategy is a noun and stands for "a plan of action designed to achieve a long-term or overall aim.

The word "strategy" is derived from the Greek word "stratçgos"; stratus (meaning army) and "ago" (meaning leading/moving).

Strategy can also be defined as "A general direction set for the company and its various components to achieve a desired state in the future. Strategy results from the detailed strategic planning process".

The strategic planning process is intended to define what needs to be done, how it will be done and who will do which part. This structured approach ensures that the same vision is implemented throughout the entire organization and not each department's version of the vision.

Earlier strategy used to be created for anywhere between 5 to 10 years, however with the corporate world in such a state of fluidity where things change overnight and in the most unpredictable manner, strategies are generally designed for 3-5 years.

Once the organization has identified where it wants to be, the next step is to start mapping out how to get there. For example, to increase market share by 5 %, separate mini strategies have to be created for increasing sales, identifying new markets and planning how to enter those markets, building operational capabilities, streamlining the supply chain, ensuring availability of funds so that raw material is available for increased production. In short, the leadership has to create a comprehensive action plan and display the ability for 360-degree thinking.

An action plan is merely a written document outlining the goals that have to be achieved, action steps to be taken, people responsible for taking those actions and detailed milestones for each action. A review plan will also be required to keep track of progress made along the desired lines.

The purpose of strategy is to outdistance yourself from the competitors by delighting customers, capturing market share and doing it in a manner that is different from the competitors. There are three components of a strategy that organizations must be very clear about.

What outcomes are we trying to achieve and what value are we trying to create for customers?

Who is our target segment and which markets do we want to target? (Also what we will not do and segments/ markets we will stay out of too is part of the strategy.)

How will we achieve market dominance and what do we want our customers to know us for?

If the entire organization has clarity about these three points, then it can be said that the organization has a clearly defined strategy. My experience of dealing with very senior levels in the organization shows that the answer to these questions will differ depending on which department head is answering them. Each department will address the questions from their functional lens and there is little common ground and shared vision within the organization.

In most organizations, there is little clarity about these issues at the top and the understanding becomes progressively hazy as you move to the mid manager levels and lower. It is usually the lack of clarity about the strategy of the organization and the outcomes that the organization wants to achieve, that leads to different departments working in silos and the visible lack of inter-department coordination.

A strategy is about allocating the scarce resources within the organizational and integrating organizational activities to meet the mid to long-term objectives of the organization. A well-thought-through approach is essential to ensure that decisions are not taken in a vacuum.

Strategy also involves clearly defining the goals to be achieved and detailed plans for achieving these goals. This would also include contingency planning to overcome the volatility and uncertainty of the current business environment. Strategy is not only about identifying where the organization wants to go but also creating an action plan for getting there. While strategy is about creating the plan, execution is implementing the action plan.

An effective strategy has the following attributes:

Strategy is important as it gives direction to the organization. In the absence of perfect foresight, organizations must be ready to deal with the uncertainties of the current business environment by clearly articulating the direction in which the organization wants to head.

Strategy deals with a mid to long-term focus rather than routine operations, it involves things like the introduction of new products, tapping into new markets, exiting certain markets, adopting new approaches in existing markets, incorporating new technologies, etc.

Strategy is moreover meant to counter the efforts of the competitors by taking into account the changing explicit and implicit needs of the customer.

I have seen many organizations make the mistake while strategizing, of assuming that the competition will sit idle while they are creating plans to disrupt the market with new ideas and approaches. They need to be cognizant of the fact, that competition is also constantly brainstorming and trying to come up with ideas that will differentiate them from their peers.

If an organization does not have a robust and well thought out strategy it will flounder in the middle to long term. A faulty strategy may not have an immediate adverse impact on business but will eventually lead to major challenges that the organization will encounter.

Some of the tools useful for creating strategy are SWOT analysis, environment scanning to identify patterns, trends, and relationships within an organization's internal and external environment, brainstorming, etc.

There are few corporate blunders as staggering as Kodak's missed break in digital photography, a technology that was invented by Kodak itself in 1975. This strategic failure was the direct cause of Kodak's decline over a decade as digital photography destroyed its film-based business model. Kodak did not fail overnight and continued to show great earnings till 2000 only to file for insolvency in 2012

How many performance management systems used by organizations currently can gauge the strategic mind-set of a manager/ leader and her contribution towards creating a robust strategy that can disrupt competition and give an edge to the organization in these competitive times.

Strategy, however, does not make money for the organization. Money is made when execution happens with excellence.

Execution:

"Ideas are yesterday, execution is today and excellence will see you into tomorrow."

– Julian Hall

Just execution is not sufficient for an organization to be competitive. What organizations need is execution excellence.

The English dictionary defines execution as carrying out a plan, order, or course of action.

And excellence as: the quality of being outstanding or extremely good

Execution is the second pillar of performance. Execution is where the action plans are converted into action and is the real test of the robustness of any strategy. Even the best strategy will fail to deliver the desired results if not implemented well.

Jamie Dimon, CEO of JPMorgan Chase, opined, **"I'd rather have a first-rate execution and second-rate strategy any time than a brilliant idea and mediocre management."** An excellent execution machinery gives the organization the privilege of bouncing off strategies and to course-correct if a strategy or action plan is found wanting in any respect.

Execution is where money is made, hence it should also be given the utmost importance, however, focusing on execution excellence at the cost of creating a robust long-term strategy and developing organizational talent can be a dangerous combination. Many great organizations of the past have paid the price of giving disproportionate importance to meeting execution targets and not keeping an eye out for the next opportunity or threat.

The world's first computer with a Windows base was invented by Xerox more than a decade before Macintosh and Windows PCs hit the market, however, the company did not make many efforts towards marketing them as their photocopiers were doing extremely well and the entire organization was focused on achieving photocopier sales targets. No one was keeping an eye out for the changing trends in the market. Eventually, Xerox realized its mistake and began marketing the Xerox Star, a graphical workstation based on technology developed for the Alto, but it was too late by then.

The failure rate for execution is very high. Leaders devote time and effort to coming up with workable plans, only to discover that the execution does not happen as planned because of so many unforeseeable and uncontrollable events.

Today speed of execution is very important, hence being right the first time is what organizations should aim for, as reworks are an avoidable expense. This would require clear communication, perfectly understood goals, availability of the required skill sets and effective monitoring to identify and eliminate errors at the earliest.

Everyone in the organizations must have clarity of goals and a detailed action plan for achieving these goals along with the commitment of team members and collaboration across teams if execution excellence is to be achieved. This is however seldom the case and that is where the role of a leader becomes very important.

When we interact with leaders we ask them how well have their team members bought into the strategy of the organization and how clear are they about their role in making it a success. We invariably get the response that every team has clarity about the organization's priorities. When we interact with team members and ask five of them to identify the one thing that they have to accomplish with excellence for the team goals to be met, we get five different answers. If the leader has done a good job of cascading the organizational strategy and goals, we should hear only one response but that seldom happens. One can't expect execution excellence in the absence of absolute clarity about team goals and how these will be achieved.

A leader's job is to ensure that everyone on the team is on the same page and has a line of sight of the goals at each level. She further has to plan for and provide the resources that are needed by the team along with removing any obstacles that the team may be facing by way of skill sets, competencies, guidance and empowerment to be able to consistently deliver with excellence.

A Harvard Business Review study brought out the fact that senior leaders ranked execution as the most desirable skill, while managers at lower levels who are responsible for executing, ranked it fourth, behind abilities like inspiring, motivating, and problem-solving. Everyone may not be aware of the paramount importance of execution excellence and it becomes the responsibility of the leaders to focus the energies of the teams towards it.

It is a known fact that execution excellence plays a very important role in creating a competitive advantage for any organization. Execution excellence is the only sustainable competitive advantage that an organization can have and this is what distinguishes successful organizations from unsuccessful ones and ensures that they stay profitable.

Execution excellence is a commitment to raise the level of productivity during execution. This means you raise the bar about how people from different teams in the organization collaborate to produce the desired business outcome by raising quality, productivity and consistency.

According to Franklin Covey leaders are good at planning but struggle with execution. They have found that organizations fail at execution because:

85% of the employees do not know what are the important goals of the company

87% of the workers do not know what to do to achieve the goals

80% of the employees do not know or track their measures of success

72% of the workers are not held accountable for their results

It doesn't matter how good your strategies are, if you don't execute with excellence it won't really matter. Steve Jobs once said, **"To me, ideas are worth nothing unless executed... Execution is worth millions".** Even the most brilliant strategy will be wasted if it is not fully realized. Thought leaders tend to focus a huge amount of energy on idea generation, they may also need to get more engaged with executing for best results.

The German field marshal, Moltke the Elder felt that "No plan survives contact with the enemy." According to him, there can be no perfect strategy. A sound strategy should be enhanced and developed during the implementation process. Some leaders start with execution and subsequently define their strategy. Strategy for them is the general direction they want to move in and not a step-by-step plan to get to their destination. This approach makes more sense in a business world that is becoming more volatile and uncertain by the day, where frequent disruption is the new normal.

Learning agility and operational agility are becoming buss words and most organizations are encouraging their employees to accept and implement change more readily. To thrive one does not have to accept or adapt to change but be a driver of change. Organizations and products that have disrupted the market have done much better than those who played it safe by bringing about incremental changes.

Agility has two components to it and only those organizations that can incorporate both as part of their execution culture are going to benefit from being agile. Agility is the ability to move fast, but it also encompasses the ability to change direction easily. True agility is the ability to change direction without losing speed. Organizations that were able to do it during the lockdown performed much better than their peers. Even those organizations that were not in favour of working from home were forced to give in to the new reality, but all did not make the transition with the same amount of effectiveness. Those who displayed agility outperformed their competitors.

One needs to think of the organization's growth as parallel to nature. If ideas are the seeds, think of execution as the water and sunlight. Without water and sunlight, a seed will never grow. So no matter how brilliant your strategy may seem at the time, an idea alone is never enough to guarantee the growth of your business -- but execution can.

The road to excellence is always under construction as there is no final state of brilliance that has to be achieved. The moment you reach the desired level of excellence you need to set yourself new goals to move to the next level. The pursuit of execution excellence is a continuous quest for improving productivity and quality. It is the belief that an organization has in the idea that there is always a better and more effective way of doing things.

One of our Japanese clients has a value, that they have pasted all over the place and is practiced by all levels in the organization. It says "Stop- Look- Act". They constantly keep taking their processes apart to take a closer look at its components, to figure out if there is a better way of executing and getting enhanced results and then they implement the same process but in a slightly better and efficient way. It could be the introduction of new technology, utilization of additional information, or the elimination of one unnecessary step that can lead to some improvement in throughput. They work on the principle of incremental improvement in processes and over some time this creates a huge competitive advantage for the organization.

One of our clients started working on projects aimed at bringing about incremental improvements in execution and has achieved massive savings in cost, time and resources over 4 years. What they have smartly done is made the efforts put on projects, part of the KRAs and KPIs of employees with heavy weightage given to the outcomes of these projects. In 2019 they won every award that their company had to offer along with a few external awards. Today the team is so charged that they come up with ideas to implement or even go ahead and implement improvement ideas and just report back the results.

This journey was not easy, we first had to engage with the employees and help them appreciate the importance of the tasks they were performing and make them understand the business impact of these tasks. The leadership had to become more engaged with the employees at every level as the projects were regularly reviewed across the country.

By the second year, the leaders took a back seat and asked the employees to come up with projects for process improvement as they were the closest to the action. Different teams were assigned projects and budgets and regular reviews were conducted by the leadership. It is an ongoing process and showing fantastic results by way of improved efficiency and reduced costs.

However, the biggest surprise was that the employee engagement scores went off the charts. For the first time, the employees at every level in that department felt engaged and empowered and had easy access to top leadership. The leaders in the department practiced servant leadership, where they assumed the responsibility of removing roadblocks and supported the different teams to achieve success.

Though there is so much more to execution the performance management systems existing in most organization only track achievements against targets hence giving a skewed picture of who the performers are. The PMS only tracks what is achieved and not how it was accomplished.

People:

The third Pillar of Performance is People or Talent to be more precise.

The dictionary defines talent as "a characteristic feature, aptitude, or disposition of a person or animal.

The good news is that though some talent is hereditary, most of it can be developed given the right environment, support and opportunities and optimising team talent is one of the most important responsibilities of leaders.

Helping talent grow and enabling it to deliver more with less is where leadership needs to focus a major part of its energy. Developing talent is not the sole responsibility of the HR department but that of the entire organization. Leaders who do a better job of managing talent need to be recognized and rewarded for their efforts.

For an organization to compete successfully in today's global marketplace, it needs to be innovative, adaptive, and agile. Achieving this depends on the skill and knowledge of the workforce. Employees need to be agile learners to see things in a new light and be ready to make the next move.

The ability to learn, unlearn and relearn has never been more important than today where changes in the business environment takes place frequently. When organizations do not support a continual process of learning, innovation retards, processes become outdated, and nothing new is ever accomplished. Learning needs to be flexible, on-demand and on a continual basis to enable superior performance.

Every organization has an HR or Human Resources department whose main purpose is to keep the organization provided with employees with the right skill sets and experience, more or less on demand. The HR department also tries to ensure that employees are not exploited and are being provided opportunities to develop their skills and competencies. HR has the added responsibility of working with below-average performers to get them to contribute more towards the goals of the organization.

As a person running a consulting company most of our interactions are with the HR heads and I feel that most organizations do not seem to appreciate the pivotal role that HR can play in the success of the organization. The HR department in most organizations is treated as "Peoples Problem Solvers" and a hiring and firing department, though HR needs to be much more than that.

I feel HR needs to be part of the senior-most decision-making team and be an active contributor to the team working on strategy. It is the HR team that will ensure that the organisation has the right talent at the right time in the right place for the organization to be able to implement its' strategy and plan expansion and diversification activities.

Henry Ford is on record to have said that people should leave their brains behind when they come to work. That may have been the right philosophy when the world was experiencing mass production for the first time and creativity on the shop floor could have resulted in chaos in an assembly line set up.

The pyramid structure worked well in the 20th century, when most of the workers were employed by manufacturing organizations and the employment contract was provisional. People were hired for being able to follow instructions and repeat actions tirelessly with minimal errors. (Today most of these tasks are performed by robots.) Leaders viewed employees simply as a cost and not as individuals who could contribute to improvements in the process through their ideas. The pyramid system does not work well in the service industry where employees are expected to be decision-makers and creative problem solvers.

Today however customers are demanding solutions and greater efficiencies from employees and the organizations along with higher standards of customer centricity as the price for staying loyal. Leaders who can create empowered and engaged team members will deliver more to clients as knowledge has become a commodity and the necessary information for good decision-making is available across every level in the organization. Unfortunately, most leaders continue to use command and control, which are management tools from the industrial age, in the Human Age, where an entrepreneur's mind-set and freedom to take decisions will deliver more.

My biggest disconnect is with the name of the HR department itself. Human Resources implies that we are still treating people as a resource. If one employee could seamlessly replace another then we would be right in considering employees as a resource. That unfortunately is not the case as each employee contributes to the team in her own unique way.

Each one of us has our own painful experience of losing a high potential employee from our team to attrition and we distinctly remember the efforts we made to try to retain that person, usually unsuccessfully. If people were a resource, we would have got a perfect fit as a replacement in the next seven days. Even if a team gets an immediate replacement for an employee that has decided to move on, it takes the new team members at least six months to start contributing at the level of the employee that left. Hence losing top talent is much more expensive than it appears on the face of it.

Employees are talent with each one of them contributing towards the team goals in their distinctive way and the loss of an employee means lost experience, contacts, client relationships and tacit knowledge which will all leave with the employee. Even the best repository maintained by the organization will not be able to capture all of it.

One of the biggest contribution a leader can make to the organization is to help in hiring, developing, growing and retaining talent. This will include capabilities like fencing-in high potentials, through interesting learning opportunities, a clear fast-tracked career path and preferential treatment to ensure that any offer from competition seems unattractive. Organizations that have such leaders will outperform their peers, irrespective of the business they are in.

I have heard many full forms of HR from employees, however, the one that I can identify with the most is "Human Remains". In most organizations HR ends up working with the Humans that "Remain" in the company despite the best or worst efforts of their managers. Where managers tend to micromanage even high performers and use leadership tools designed for the industrial age even today when we are well into the Human Age.

HR should be instrumental in creating the right work culture in the organization by encouraging certain behaviours and penalizing others. Creating a culture that engages and empowers employees should be their main agenda.

Jack Welch as chairman and CEO of GE was named the Manager of the Century by Fortune Magazine in 1999. He was credited with transforming GE from a company that was into appliances and lightbulbs into a multinational corporation that successfully ventured into financial services and media as well as industrial products.

His recommendation to leaders was to focus on people issues and to get the people-related decisions right. In an HRB article on the topic of hiring right, he observed that **"executives spend more time on managing people and making people decisions than on anything else — and they should. No other decisions are so long-lasting in their consequences or so difficult to unmake."** In the years he was heading GE, he probably spent more than half his time getting the right people in the right places and then helping them succeed. He would involve himself in hiring decisions, something that most CEOs tend to delegate to others in their team.

He had proposed that any leader involved in on-boarding or promoting employees be scored on the successes or failure of such employees – what he had termed as their "batting average." He noted that this would not only help to assess someone's critical selection skills but also encourage bosses to support new hires or undo poor appointments at the earliest. He felt that the leader should not have the privilege of saying "I promoted - she failed" instead it should be "I promoted - we failed". This would put more pressure on the bosses to hire right and ensure that the employee was given enough support in her march to success.

He held that the team with the best players wins--and leaders should expend their energy and time in evaluating, coaching, and building the self-confidence of team members. Jack believed that **"People development should be a daily event, integrated into every aspect of your regular goings-on."**

The consistent development of great leaders is essential for the long-term success of an organization, yet organizations often overlook it or haphazardly undertake leadership development with sporadic talent development engagements thrown in for team members.

Great leaders regularly take stock of their team's talent balance sheet and have clarity about the capability, contribution and potential of all team members and they spend their time and energy providing them with opportunities to hone their skills and improve. Leaders who can create more leaders will constantly add more value to their organization than those who focus only on meeting monthly targets.

The performance management systems followed by most organizations, however, give disproportionate importance to execution as that is the only thing tracked by the system. The focus is only on the achievement of goals and targets. The same amount of importance is not given to evaluating the process of target achievement. This is partly because it is easier to monitor target achievement than to track the softer skills like strategic thinking and the ability to work with and through people. An effective performance management system should access an employee's contribution across all three pillars of performance, which are Strategy, Execution and Talent Development.

The definition of good performance changes as a person moves up the corporate value chain and leaders need to understand how their roles evolve during an employee's journey from being an individual contributor to a manager of people and a manager of managers and so on.

Let us quickly recap the purpose of business to have clarity about the significance of each pillar of performance at different levels in the organization.

We are clear that every business is in the business of making money through the creation of satisfied customers. Strategy is an idea or a plan for the organization to achieve its vision and goals. If the strategy is faulty the organization will suffer in the mid to long term. Strategy however does not make money for a company.

Money is made when execution happens with excellence. If execution is below par the company will not make much money irrespective of how great the strategy is. If execution is faulty the impact will be faced immediately and if corrective action is not taken urgently the organization can go under.

Finally, it is the people who create the strategy and execute it with excellence. They are also the ones who create the team and organizational culture, which is extremely important for the success or failure of an organization in the long term.

Tom Smith in his exemplary book "Change the Culture, Change the Game" states the organizations are designed to succeed or fail in the long run depending on their organizational culture. According to him, culture produces results. How many Performance Management systems track a leaders' contribution to creating a positive culture in the organization?

Every person in the organization works along the three pillars of performance, namely Strategy, Execution and People. However, the time and energy spent on each of these pillars will depend on one's role. The figure below will help you understand this concept:

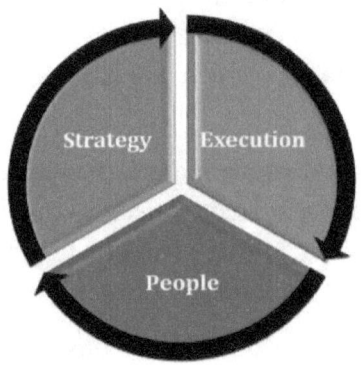

	IC	Jr. Manager	Sr. Managers
Execution	85%	40%	20%
People	10%	30%	40%
Strategy	5%	30%	40%

In the above image, we can see that though the different levels in the organization, all work across the same three pillars, however, the amount of time and energy they spend on each of the pillars of performance is different for every level.

We can call an Individual Contributor (IC) a high performer if she can achieve her targets while spending 85% of her time on execution, focusing on meeting weekly, monthly and yearly targets. Any training provided to her should be technical or functional and should help her achieve her targets.

At the IC level an employee will need to spend 10 % of time and energy interacting with others while seeking and providing help and minimizing conflicts. She should possess some people skills as she would need to collaborate with her team members and engage with her manager.

Though she may not be contributing towards organizational strategy she needs to spend some time and energy (5 % in this case) on understanding what the organization's strategy is and how her role contributes towards the achievement of this strategy. If this linkage is not established in the mind of the IC where will the motivation to perform her tasks with excellence come from? The IC should not only be aware of the tasks that they perform but also the business impact of these tasks.

When a person becomes a manager, though while she continues to work across the same three pillars, her priorities need to shift, with more time and energy devoted to mid to long-term planning and effectively managing talent, instead of focusing only on pure execution. Though execution and meeting targets is more important for the manager than the IC, it should be accomplished through reviews, follow-up, developing capabilities and hand-holding, rather than through hands-on execution.

A senior manager or a leader will need to spend even more time and energy than a manager on strategic activities like identifying future market trends and red flagging future threats well in time. They also need to be ready to grab potential opportunities and disrupt competitors.

Senior managers and leaders will also have to devote more time and effort to people-related activities as their sphere of engagement and the ability to impact results is much greater.

Though the numbers mentioned in the table above are not cast in stone, the shift towards strategic thinking and people development is mandatory for a manager or leader to stay relevant.

An individual contributor needs to complete assigned tasks within stipulated timelines and with the required quality standard. For accomplishing this she will have to be punctual, quality conscious and reliable and will have to manage her time and plan her daily schedule to minimise slippages and inefficiencies.

A Manager of People, on the other hand, has to plan about assigning work, mentoring and coaching team members, measuring and reviewing the output of others. They also need to remove obstacles that their team members may be facing in trying to deliver results. They need to recognize and reward above-average performance to motivate and energise team members.

A Manager of managers needs to assign managerial and leadership work to first-time managers. Ensuring that they have robust review processes in place. It is not only what their managers are achieving but how they are managing their teams becomes very important as they have little direct visibility of activities on the front line. The manager of managers needs to be good at spotting trends and asking questions rather than providing answers.

Functional managers have all the deliverables of managers of managers along with the additional responsibilities of creating long-term functional strategies and looking for a sustainable competitive advantage rather than just an immediate but temporary edge.

Business managers who head the entire business vertical are responsible for meeting quarterly profit targets, and focus on things like market share, product introduction, and manpower targets, identifying markets to enter or exit depending on the potential of the market and at the same time have a line of sight of goals three to five years into the future.

Each level in the organization needs to look at their role and responsibilities and figure out if they are managing their energies most productively.

While working across the same three pillars of performance the responsibilities and deliverables are very different at each level in the organization.

It is very dangerous when all levels in the organizations start focusing only on execution and celebrate the achievement of monthly and yearly targets, at the cost of strategic planning and talent acquisition and development.

Great organizations like Kodak, Nokia, HMT, Xerox that were too focused on execution and meeting yearly targets, missed out completely on identifying future market trends and threats, which finally led to their collapse.

The second challenge is that most organizations equate performance that a person displays with the potential that she possesses.

I would request you to take a closer look at the Performance Management system deployed in your organization. Does it capture the contribution of each employee across Strategy, Execution and People - the three pillars of performance or does it mainly focus on target achievement? A distorted measurement system will lead to warped behaviours as only what gets measured gets managed.

If your organization is in the business of making money shouldn't value addition by way of strategic ideas and increasing the human capital also be part of the measurements to gauge true performance. You may have managers/leaders who achieve their targets consistently using carrot and stick or command and control. These people on paper show that they have achieved targets but at what costs? Did they generate more profits for the organization? As hidden costs like attrition, rehiring, inducting, and training if not correctly apportioned can lead to a distorted understanding of who the real contributors are.

Let me share a few examples of defects in the performance management system that quite a few organizations may have. They measure incorrect parameters or do not measure at all the most important parameters.

I was the Training Head in an ITES company and my department was measured basis the number of workshops we conducted, the feedback scores we achieved, which included content quality, the relevance of the content, the efficacy of the training and the different parameters regarding delivery quality. We were also however accountable for the number of employees we trained during the month.

A typical training rollout would look something like this. The topic of the workshop would be decided in consultation with the line managers, the enrolments for the program would open two weeks in advance and within seven days all 20 slots would be filled. On the day of the training, however, just 5 people would show up. Repeated calls and pleading by my team members would increase the attendance to maybe eight participants.

The standard response from line managers would be that there was a spike at work and they could not spare the people for the session. Though the feedback about the program would be great, my team would still get slaughtered in the monthly review process.

In my next review with the CEO, I pointed out to him that I was being reviewed for something that was beyond my control. I should be reviewed on things like quality, efficacy, relevance, quality of delivery and not attendance. The CEO saw the logic and made training attendance part of the line manager's KRA and overnight we had a full house with requests for accommodating a couple of extra guys and the training budget was being effectively utilized, and the training team became star performers. The line managers who were initially underplaying the importance of training sessions became our advocates and aggressively sold the training programs to their team members.

Please remember, only what is measured can be managed and most performance management systems are flawed as they do not track the critical contribution of employees. It is the responsibility of the leadership to design a performance management system that captures true performance and not just target achievement.

In the last organization I worked, I carried sales targets and also delivered workshops, was an assessor and conducted coaching and mentoring sessions. On average I would be either traveling or delivering sessions 15 days a month. A schedule like this left me with only 7 working days to achieve my monthly sales targets. Though I had fantastic team members who were experts in what they did and were also willing to stretch, my absence still made a difference to order closures.

In our weekly meeting, we were reviewed on achievement against the targets provided, which were designation or band based and not based on the territory available or it's potential so there could be 5 people competing in one geographical area while an entire region was allotted to someone else. The other challenge with this system was that though each person beyond a certain level was supposed to deliver 5 workshops every month, most people could not do so. I on the other hand ended up spending 15 days in delivery and 7 days on business development.

Repeated efforts to make the country manager understand the fault in the design of the PMS fell on deaf years as by her standards the only thing that mattered to the company was the billing done in that month. The system was only measuring execution against yearly targets. How it was done, by whom and at what cost, was not tracked and people not meeting their delivery commitments were also not called out.

Finally, I put my foot down and did only 5 days of delivery which was usually only for my clients. This came as a rude shock for most people as they could not meet their sales targets despite orders in the pipeline and soured my relations with my manager and peers, which made it easier to decide to start my own consulting company in 2014.

As I was the backbone of the delivery process I stayed on as an associate for six months with a minimum number of guaranteed days of work. What worked for me was that as a consultant I was charging multiple times my daily CTC to the company, as an employee, I had no business development commitments and it gave me ample time to develop a pipeline of new clients for my company on my free days.

My contract was renewed on even better terms for another six months beyond which I declined as I had developed my pipeline of clients and the organization had created its delivery capabilities.

The point to be noted in this example is that only billing was being tracked every month and no one was able to calculate the adverse impact of measuring only execution, on profitability, nor chart out a course where the actual contribution of employees could be measured. As we are in the business of making money equating performance with only execution can be suicidal and not measuring the true contribution of each employee can also leave the workforce demotivated.

As we work with organizations across industries we have noticed that employees are most demotivated just after the review process is completed. Most employees are dissatisfied as they feel they have not been assessed correctly and this is mainly because of the defect in the performance management systems that most organizations have in place.

In the last chapter, I would like to make some suggestions to sort out this mess, but it would require both HR and line managers to work closely and create a new system that tracks not only target achievement but the overall contribution of an employee.

Chapter 4

Perception

Berelson and Steiner in their book Human behaviour, define perception as the complex process by which people select and organize sensory stimulation into a meaningful and rational picture of the world. No two people will perceive a situation in the same way. Still, perception is too significant an issue to be left to others. If we are aware of the importance of how people perceive us only then will we spend the time and energy required to manage other's perceptions about us. People will always form perceptions about who we really are so it is advisable to manage the process. If we don't create a perception about us as leaders by design, it will anyways get created by default.

A simple example would be of a leader who is naturally reserved and does not like to engage with team members and peers, unless it is related to work or when it is essential for her to reach out to people. Unfortunately, such a leader may be perceived to be either snobbish, secretive, or a person with a personal agenda. That may not be the reality as far as the leader is concerned but it is what the team members perceive her to be.

People form perceptions about others based on their actions and about themselves based on their intent. As the team members are not aware of the leader's intent or motivations, they only look at behaviours and form a perception about her.

Managers and leaders in an organization are entrusted with team members and peers who they must work with and through their combined efforts realize organizational objectives. Each one of us, especially Managers/Leaders are on stage all the time. Employees observe everything we say and do and form their perceptions about us. One might turn around and say "this is only their perception about me, but I am not really like that". One needs to understand that their perception of you, is their reality as far as you are concerned.

We have all heard the adage "The first impression is the last impression." It is not entirely true, as when faced with substantial evidence to the contrary we do change our impression about people. A more accurate statement would be "The first impression is a lasting impression." Perceptions have stickiness and once formed; we do not change our perceptions easily. One needs to put in a lot of effort to change the perception of people once it is formed. Therefore, it is pertinent that people perceive us the way we want to be perceived, in the first instance itself.

The perception people form about us is based on the interactions we have with them, the experiences we give them and on the quality of communication we have with others. If we can manage these interactions, proactively, we can also manage the perceptions that people form about us.

The very fact that you are reading this book gives me the impression that you would like to tap into your "Leadership Potential". That makes it very important for you to understand the basic difference between a manager and a leader.

Just because a person is in the top two bands of the organization does not automatically make her a leader. It just means that the organization expects you to display leadership qualities at this level. I have met very senior people in organizations, supposedly in leadership roles, who are actually excellent managers and they achieve their targets by managing the environment around them using their designation and authority to get the tasks done.

On the net one will get plenty of templates highlighting the differences between a manager and a leader:

Sample 1:

Managers Vs Leaders	
Managers	Leaders
Focus on things	Focus on People
Do things right	Do the right things
Plan	Inspire
Organize	Influence
Direct	Motivate
Control	Build
Follow rules	Shape entities

Sample 2:

The Distinction between Managers and Leaders: Functions and Approach	
Managers	**Leaders**
• Organise	• Innovate
• Plan	• Visionary
• Accept responsibility	• Seek responsibility
• Control employees and functions	• Creative
• Specialise	• Entrepreneurial
• Minimize risk	• Flexible
• Set goals	• Calculated risk taker
• Delegate cautiously	• Decision maker
• Motivate	• Set challenging goals
• Co-ordinate	• Seek followers
• Delegate	• Seek excitement

Though there is nothing wrong with these differentiators between a Manager and a Leader, it comes across to me as more of semantics than the actual difference between the two entities.

Let us try to simplify the differences between the traits of a manager and a leader to something actionable. The three most important differences between a Manager and a Leader are:

- While a manager uses his authority to get the job done a leader has moral authority over team members and peers.

- Team members do a Manager's bidding because they have to, as not following instructions can lead to unpleasant repercussions. In the case of the leader, however, team members and peers display the required behaviour because they want to. They have bought into the idea and now they own it.

- Any person who has a team can be a manager and can also deliver spectacular results while you can only be a leader in the true sense if people willingly follow you.

As the manager gets her authority from her designation one has to attain certain seniority in the organization before she can really start leveraging her power, while leadership can be displayed by any person at any level in the organizations. In our interactions with various organizations in the corporate world, we still come across a lot of managers who are designated as leaders by their organizations.

Trustworthiness is the most important attribute that a leader needs to display. We are watchful of people we don't trust and are very unlikely to follow them willingly. Unfortunately, the corporate world does not seem to have realised the importance of trust in the success of a leader.

Earlier trust was treated as a value that people possessed and displayed, but Steven MR Covey in his thought-provoking book, "The Speed of Trust" has described trust as a "must-have" competency for any leader. He claims that without the majority of the people trusting you, one can at best be an effective manager but never a true leader.

According to the Harvard Business Research Management Review **"...the foundation of a great workplace is created by organizational credibility, respect and fairness which form the foundation of trust."**

The trust that leaders place in those they lead allows both the leader and her followers to excel. It is not possible to create engaged and empowered employees without ample trust being displayed by the leader as well as the followers. Along the way leaders and their followers, will make mistakes; however, an honest and caring approach will allow those mistakes to be resolved seamlessly.

A survey done by Office Vibes about the benefits of trust at the workplace throws up the following data:

- Trust in the workplace helps with handling change.

- Trust has the potential to decrease stress by 74% and reduce burnout.

- Teams that trust their managers have a 76% higher level of employee engagement.

- Trust in the workplace enables creativity and innovation.

- Trusting relationships are at the base of successful difficult conversations.

For the above-mentioned reasons, it becomes imperative that a leader gives sufficient attention and energy in creating a trusting environment that encourages true engagement and empowerment. A leader must also focus on being perceived as trustworthy herself if she wants to succeed in the long run.

Before we start building this competency, we need to clearly understand what trust is.

Trust is:

- My faith in your ability or word in some specific area

- Trust means that you will communicate with me in an honest manner and will not have any hidden agenda

- Trust includes the degree to which I believe you will look out for my best interest

- Trust means that you care about my welfare and success and will help me achieve my goals

I am sure we have worked with leaders who display the above-mentioned traits and also with others who don't. Just ask yourself in which scenario were you more productive and energised and less stressed while working towards delivering organisational goals.

- Productive relations are based on trust – often unrecognized and taken for granted

- Trust is a resource that increases with use

- Trust enables coordination without coercion

- Trust facilitates in driving change initiatives

Isn't it surprising that in most organizations it is not leaders but managers who get promoted to senior positions and the reason for that is our skewed performance management systems that don't factor in the softer aspects of leadership and focus only on targets being met as the criteria for superior performance. This comes at a cost as at some point in time real leaders may attrite from the organization, and the different teams in the organization may get demotivated and disillusioned. Low trust organizations do not perform well over the long run as collaboration, risk-taking and problem-solving cannot be accomplished effectively in a low trust environment.

"In low trust groups, interpersonal relationships interfere with and distort the perception of the problem. Energy and creativity are diverted from finding comprehensive, realistic solutions and members use the problem as an instrument to minimize their vulnerability. In contrast, in high trust groups there is less socially generated uncertainty and problems are solved more effectively."

– Zand

In low trust groups, less time is spent on getting to the root cause of the problem and finding a workable solution and more time is consumed in pinning the blame on someone. In high trust groups, just the opposite is witnessed.

If a leader has to be willingly followed by team members and peers she has to be perceived above all things as a person who can be trusted. But the challenge with trust is that it is built incrementally during a long period, over the various interactions one has with others. On the other hand, it takes only one instance to destroy trust.

Let us look at something that we shall call a trust account. Every time a leader displays trustworthy behaviour towards a team member, peer, or stakeholder, a certain amount is credited to her trust account. Let us assume that the amount deposited is INR 100 per interaction. A leader displays behaviour that creates trust on five occasions and has a trust balance of INR500/- with a team member. In the sixth interaction, the leader shows deceitful behaviour which is caught out by the team member. Will the trust balance go down by INR 100 or a different amount? In all probability, the trust balance after the 6th interaction will either be zero or there may even be a negative balance in the trust account.

It takes 20 years to build a reputation and five minutes to ruin it. If you think about that, you'll do things differently.

– Warren Buffet

This means that a leader cannot choose to display trustworthy behaviour on Mondays, Wednesdays, and Fridays and the balance days of the week, behave whichever way she wants. Such a leader will always have a negative trust balance. This also means that one can't fake being trustworthy. One will have to become trustworthy to be perceived as one. No one can keep up an act forever without other people seeing through their crooked designs. **"You cannot fool all the people all the time"**

The reason why I am focusing only on being perceived as a trustworthy leader is that trust covers all the bases needed for great leadership. To be perceived as trustworthy a leader will have to learn to deliver in the following three areas repeatedly and with excellence as these are the three main pillars of Trust.

Competency Trust:

A leader who is not perceived as competent will not have people following her willingly. She will be forced to use her authority to get people to toe the line. If she is not delivering above average results through her team she may be perceived as an ineffective or inefficient leader.

A leader needs to be knowledgeable about her area of business even though she may not be an expert. In case it is a new line of business that the organization has got into, she will have to put in the efforts required to learn about it. Competence does not mean that you are the best in the team in everything, as genuine leaders are inclined to hire and work with people smarter than themselves.

Today for the first time in human history, knowledge has become a commodity and is freely available to anyone who is a seeker. Leaders will likely have people reporting to them who are better than them at some skill or process. Leveraging this talent without getting insecure is a sign of competence. A leader also needs to be aware of her strength and weakness, as leaders who are blind to their own faults but have a heightened sense of their strengths find few willing followers.

In the knowledge worker age, another sign of competence is the ability to come up with better results through collaboration and cooperation, where all inputs are valued and the contribution of others is openly acknowledged.

In our interactions with leaders in organizations, we normally ask them how open are they to ideas from others, especially junior members of the teams and if they use brainstorming as a tool for finding solutions. In most cases the answer to both these questions is in the affirmative.

We also ask them that if we were to walk into one of these brainstorming sessions will we be able to figure out, in the first five minutes, who is senior and who is junior in the group? If the answer to this question is also a yes, then the brainstorming session is a waste of time and the views of the senior-most or the most influential person in the group will finally prevail. The views of this person should be mailed as a mandate for the team to follow to save time.

The ability to learn from mistakes and course-correct are also signs of competence.

A leader is not a person who can do the work better than his men; he is a person who can get his men to do the work better than he can.

– Frederick W. Smith

Do you display the traits of competency trust currently? If not, then you need to work out an action plan where people see these behaviours from you consistently. As a leader, your competence is measured based on your ability to work through people to achieve organizational goals.

Communication Trust:

At the most elementary level, communication is the transmission of information between a sender and a receiver. But there is much more to communication that makes it effective. Your tone, attitude and actions give additional meaning to your spoken and written communications. They give people information about your temperament, opinion, or mood regardless of the words, you have used to communicate the message.

Effective communication and effective leadership are closely interwoven. As a leader, you need to be an accomplished communicator in countless situations that you face every day. You need to set expectations, share information, provide feedback, coach and mentor, motivate and drive your team members in a particular direction, among a host of other things.

As an effective leader, you need visibility for yourself through the way you communicate. Don't use only emails as they are the most ineffective form of communication for leaders. Be amongst your team members, be present, visible and available if you want people to connect with you. Learn to create visibility for yourself by interacting purposefully with your stakeholders. You must be out there in the middle of things if you expect people to follow you. They can't follow you if they can't find you and the only interaction with you is through emails.

During our coaching interactions with demotivated and disgruntled employees we often come across this trend where employees who think they are contributing hugely to achieving organizational goals, feel that they have been overlooked for promotions. As we dig deeper it becomes abundantly clear to both of us that active communication was the reason for this situation, as the person was expecting only her work to speak for itself without bothering to create visibility for herself with her manager and other stakeholders.

Leaders need to communicate clearly and frequently using different formats. Failing to do so will create the perception that the leader is detached or not involved in the happenings around her. Detachment on most occasions is interpreted as arrogance even if that is not the case. Make the time to genuinely engage with people.

For a leader over communication is a safer option than under communication. However, you have to ensure that the communication is relevant for the receiver and adds some value to their role.

Most of us tend to forget that listening is also a major part of communication. Great leaders are good at listening to ideas and building on them while giving credit to the original contributor. This makes one come across as a leader who is not insecure and open to ideas and suggestions irrespective of where they come from. Remember that all of us think better than each of us and leaders who are open to suggestions from others across different levels in the organization, normally demonstrate 360-degree thinking in their solutions.

A few other things that a leader will have to do well are as follows:

Share information proactively. Employees don't trust leaders who hold back information or when they get the news, not from their boss but the grapevine. It creates the perception that the leader does not trust her team members.

Proactively sharing bad news. Some managers think they are doing their team members a favour by not disclosing, till the last moment, news that is going to impact team members adversely. This destroys the leader's credibility. Let us assume that there are going to be 50 layoffs in the organization. Not sharing this information will cause more harm than good as the grapevine could inflate the number of redundant employees to 500, causing even good contributors to start looking out for other options.

Admit mistakes as no one expects a leader to be infallible, however concealing mistakes or glossing over them does extreme damage to the image of the leader.

Another communication skill that a leader has to master is the art of not only giving effective feedback but also displaying the capacity to ask for feedback and to work on it. The last company I worked for had a culture where team members blocked the calendar of their manager to take feedback at the end of a project and then gave feedback to the manager, about what the manager could have done better while leading the team.

Another behaviour that is very important for creating the right perception for a leader is the ability to maintain confidentiality.

The Interact/ Harris Poll of 1000 US workers shows the following results:

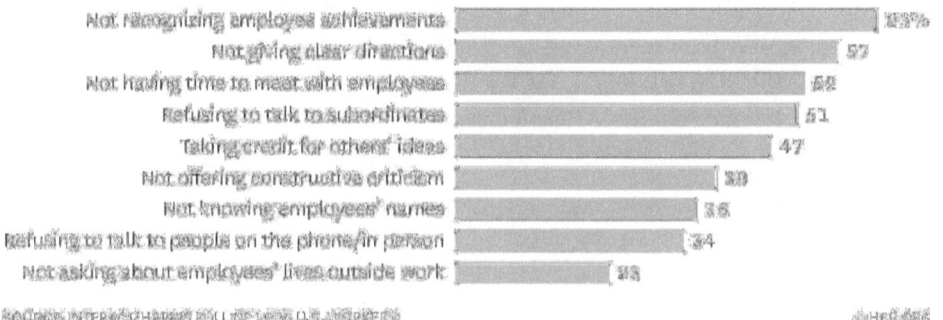

So you can see for yourself, a leader will have to work on many fronts in the communication space if she wants to be perceived as a trustworthy leader who has moral authority over her team members and peers.

Character Trust:

Character Trust is where the maximum amount of trust can be built or wrecked. People who want to be considered as great leaders will have to give the following traits their undivided attention as the maximum amount of damage to a leader's reputation can be caused if she is found wanting in any of these.

To be regarded as a leader one will always have to walk the talk and not only when it is convenient. If people hear one thing from the leader and see another, then credibility is destroyed. People need to trust you. Your behaviour and actions communicate a world of information to your team members who are constantly observing you and drawing their own conclusions regarding your trustworthiness.

The team members and peers will trust a leader who they know will not take advantage of their vulnerability and will work in their best interest. How many of us have worked with managers and leaders who always had our "good" at heart? Even corrective feedback is usually taken in the right spirit and worked upon if we know the intent is to help us get better and not find fault or humiliate.

Being deeply honest is another characteristic that is invaluably in building trust. The ability to say what you mean, to be direct and not hide behind complexity is important for a leader. Honesty is one of the most powerful tools for building trust between two people.

However, there is something that is even more powerful than honesty and that is integrity. While honesty is **"saying what you do"**, Integrity is **"doing what you say"**. To be trusted one must deliver on one's commitment every time. Over-commitment and underperformance or making false promises only to get out of a sticky situation are things that cause immense damage to a leader's reputation.

The price of being perceived as untrustworthy is immense. People don't leave organizations; they leave managers who they think do not have their best interest at heart. The team members hold back information and don't contribute ideas and question every action of the leader. No one enjoys work if you have to keep looking over your shoulder all the time and where employees are discouraged from sharing ideas and concepts and have to speak with caution as any word can be used out of context to skew the message.

Just imagine the loss of time and effort in managing expectations in an environment where trust is not high. Even then most organizations and leaders do not score high on trustworthiness. Trustworthiness is something that has a major impact on the profitability of the organization but the performance management systems don't track this trait.

The reason we chose Trust as the benchmark for managing perception is that it covers all the traits that an effective and trustworthy leader needs to display. The other thing about being trustworthy is that it cannot be faked. Either you are trustworthy or you are not. It is not possible to fake intent as it is revealed through our actions, communication, choices and behaviours. If you want to be perceived as a trustworthy leader, you will have to become one. There are no shortcuts and tricks available in this department.

Does this mean that a shy person or an introvert or someone who is not very comfortable engaging with people can never have the potential to be a leader? The answer is no. If she is willing to work on the areas that need development, she can also tap into her leadership potential. She will have to learn certain skills and behaviours that are essential for her success and here I suggest a very simple formula to bring about the necessary change.

"Fake it till you make it" It might sound counterintuitive or shallow but if you look at it closely, any skill that you have acquired has been through this method. A person who knows swimming today does so as at some point in time in the past she got into the water and pretended to be a swimmer. If she faked it long enough she slowly learnt how to swim. A certain number of people may have stopped faking after some time and they still don't know how to swim. That is how we learnt cycling also and the longer we faked, the better we got at it till one day we were confident enough to go riding at will even on congested roads.

The introvert manager or leader will have to start engaging with people even if it does not come naturally to her. She will have to start creating visibility for herself through projects, imparting training and engaging with stakeholders at all levels, even if her heart is not into it. She may have to fake the first few engagements, but over time she will become comfortable with the spotlights being focused on her and that will become her second nature. To get centre stage from the periphery will take a certain amount of effort, but it is doable.

Chapter 5

Personality

Extrovert Bass' theory of leadership states that there are three basic ways to explain how people become leaders. These theories are:

The traits theory: Some personality traits may elevate people naturally into leadership roles.

The great events theory: A crisis or important event may cause a person to rise to the occasion, which brings out extraordinary leadership qualities in an ordinary person.

The transformational leadership theory: People can choose to become leaders. People can learn and practice leadership skills.

The most favoured leadership theory today is the transformational leadership theory which states that anyone willing to put in the hard work can become a leader by acquiring the skills necessary for the role of a leader.

The dictionary definition of personality is the collection of emotional and behavioural traits that characterize a person. Your personality is how others experience you.

Is your personality important for leadership effectiveness? The answer is a definite "YES". Your public persona is the catalyst for attracting followers for your cause. Dysfunctional personality traits will drive people away making it impossible for a person to be a genuine leader.

Each one of us has a unique combination of personality dimensions. Sometimes, it can feel that one personality type might be superior to another or may fast-track one's career in an organization. However, this may not be entirely true as if you look around you will notice a lot of dissimilarity amongst the top corporate leaders globally.

Our personality does have an impact on many areas of our life. It can control how we interact with our family, friends, and spouse and can also play an important role in our effectiveness as leaders. Personality drives our automatic or natural reactions in any situation. Though it is difficult to change one's personality, it can be done if one so desires and is willing to do the heavy lifting necessary to bring about this change.

Most people mellow down naturally as they age but we can also change our personality intentionally if we want to, though it will not happen overnight. Initially one will have to adapt one's behaviour to match the situation and gradually with practice it will become second nature. Any personality trait that is coming in the way of one being an effective leader, can be toned down or modified. The fact is that most effective leaders, even 'natural' leaders like Richard Branson or PepsiCo's Indira Nooyi have had to work hard to manage their personality traits to get where they are today.

Influential leadership is a key to the success of an organization. Organizations regard great leaders as an asset and reward them with high salaries and perks. To emerge as an influential leader isn't easy as it takes time to add the requisite experiences, skills, knowledge, expertise and behavioural traits. Countless personality traits distinguish us from one another, some inherited while others are learned and we can't pin leadership potential to any specific personality traits. If you look around you will notice corporate leaders who differ tremendously from one another as far as personality traits are concerned.

There may be no template for personality traits that make a great leader but research has shown that certain personality traits do come in handy when leading people and achieving results. The higher a leader goes up the corporate ladder, the more she is scrutinized, so a demanding self-management of personality traits becomes essential to her success.

Researchers have found that the overall performance of the team is affected by the leader's personality. Followers tend to work harder for leaders who display certain personality traits. A study performed by Foushee, Chidester, Helmreich (1991), found that flight crews' performance was directly related to the captain's personality. Crew, flying with a captain who was emotionally stable, affable, and self-assured, were better able to stand up to the stress and pressure of flying and made fewer errors. However, crews who had captains who were intimidating or passive-aggressive made greater errors and performed poorly.

Followers use their observation to decide if you are an honourable and trusted leader or a self-serving person who misuses authority to look good in the eyes of her bosses. Self-serving leaders are not as effective because their subordinates only obey, not follow them. From such team members, you can expect compliance at best but never commitment in pursuit of organizational goals. Such leaders succeed in some areas because they present a good image to their seniors at the expense of their team members.

Some people feel that extroverts are more effective leaders. Introverts, on the other hand, are commonly pigeon-holed as more comfortable with ideas than with people. However, either style can be successful, as each of these styles has its merits, and different situations may call on the strengths of either approach. You need to emphasize the positives of your natural style and mitigate the drawbacks. One can also adapt one's behaviour with practice to meet a particular situation.

Extensive research done by various research organizations and groups has thrown up a list of personality traits that most successful leaders display.

While successful leaders may not exhibit all the leadership skills, mentioned below, all good leaders leverage at least some — or most — of these traits.

These personality traits make up the backbone of leadership across different levels in the organization, industries, and roles. Without these personality traits, true leadership is impossible. However, any personality trait displayed in excess will also be counterproductive.

People like to work with leaders who are calm and composed even in a crisis. Being composed can communicate professionalism but to be too composed can be perceived as being low on emotions, overly confident, or being laid back and lacking a sense of urgency. However, being too reactive or impatient can lead to the opposite conclusion.

Leadership isn't an end in itself, but a journey. It's something that you'll have to work at regularly throughout your career, regardless of which level you reach in your organization, hence the ability to learn new things becomes a must-have trait for leaders. Learning to develop new skills and personality traits is an expectation from leaders if they are to stay relevant.

Listed below are some of the personality traits that make leaders successful in the long run. These are traits that followers expect their leaders to possess and display

Learning Agility:

A personality trait that is very important today and needs to be displayed by leaders and managers at every level in the organization is that of learning agility. In today's volatile business environment, leaders can no longer rely on strategies that have worked in the past or even those that are successful currently.

Great leaders thrive on change and relish uncertainty. These individuals are displaying the trait of 'learning agility'. People who have high levels of learning agility seek out and learn from new experiences and then apply those learnings to address the next previously unexperienced situation.

Learning agility helps them find a way out when they don't know what to do.

Research by Korn Ferry has shown that **"learning agility is now the single best predictor of executive success, above intelligence and education. There are no absolutes, but agile learners tend to get promoted faster and achieve more".**

When we think of intelligence, we might think of having a lot of knowledge about different subjects. But you also need to consider quick thinking and the ability to reason and coming up with workable solutions as intelligence. Such factors represent what psychologists refer to as "crystallized" intelligence and "fluid intelligence".

Intelligence is more than simply the accumulation of facts. It also encompasses the ability to learn new things. Fluid intelligence refers to the ability to reason and think malleably. Crystallized intelligence, on the other hand, refers to the accumulation of knowledge, facts, and skills that are acquired through education and experiences.

As children, we have very little crystallised intelligence but plenty of fluid intelligence. As we grow up however our crystallised intelligence keeps increasing but our fluid intelligence shrinks. Hence we are seldom able to come up with out-of-the-box ideas as adults. We need the ability to increase our crystallised intelligence without allowing our fluid intelligence to reduce, as that is the need of the hour in a world that is changing at an ever-increasing pace.

Learning agility is not so much about what someone has accomplished. It's about what they have the potential to accomplish, especially when faced with new situations and challenges. Agile learners are creators. Sir Richard Branson used the agility mind-set to build businesses in music, telecommunications, air and rail transportation and even space travel. His biggest motivation is to keep challenging himself.

"I see life almost like one long university education that I never had

– Sir Richard Branson

Those who can embrace the new normal of rapid and constant change will stand the best chance of survival. Those who can lead and model the way for others will be in high demand. Those who can create an organizational culture based on innovation, renewal, and confidence will thrive and flourish. This is what leaders of today have to work towards to succeed.

Integrity:

"The supreme quality for leadership is unquestionably integrity. Without it, no real success is possible, no matter whether it is on a section gang, a football field, in an army, or in an office."

– Dwight D. Eisenhower

The importance of integrity should be obvious. Though it may not necessarily be measured in employee evaluations, integrity is essential for a leader to succeed in an organization. It's especially important for top-level executives who are deciding the direction for the organization and making countless other important decisions. Research shows that integrity may be a potential blind spot for organizations.

"Companies with strong, ethical management teams enhance their ability to attract investors, customers and talented professionals," explains Tim Hird, adding that ethical behaviour should start at the top and the leadership should proactively work towards creating a culture that values integrity.

Leaders are judged by their reports and peers on their competence and character. A major part of character is integrity and signals if the leader can be trusted or not. A leader who has competence and integrity is a very valuable asset for organizations in the medium to long term and is more effective than a leader who lacks these two traits. However, most performance management systems either do not measure this trait or do not give it the importance it deserves.

As integrity is so important, organizations need to define behaviours that are ethical and desirable and those that are unethical and should be avoided and leaders must be measured on these behaviours at the time of their review.

Behaviours like honesty, fair treatment of employees, acknowledging the contributions of others, owning up to mistakes and accepting that others will also make mistakes should be encouraged as it will create a culture of ethical behaviour in the organization.

Effective Communication:

The earlier definition of effective communication is not valid today. Earlier communication was about a sender, a receiver and a medium used to convey the message, followed by a feedback loop. It was believed if the other person understood what you were conveying, communication was effective. Not anymore. Today communication is considered effective only if you get the desired results.

Effective leadership demands engaging with people in a way that motivates and energizes them. This requires communicating in a manner that goes beyond just relaying information to them. The most successful leaders inspire others, build connections between people, influence their decisions, and create synergies throughout the organization.

A leader is someone who inspires positive change by encouraging those around them to work toward a common objective. A leader's most powerful tool for doing so is the ability to influence others. Effective communication becomes vital to influence, gain the trust of others, align efforts in the pursuit of organizational goals, and inspire positive change.

When communication is ineffective none of the above objectives can be achieved. Ineffective communication leads to a situation where important information can be misinterpreted, causing relationships to suffer and, ultimately, creating barriers that hinder progress.

Self-Awareness:

Being self-aware enables leaders to leverage their strengths and work on their limitations. Having a clear understanding of one's capabilities and limitations also allows for more effective interactions, because a self-aware leader displays more emotional intelligence and can recognize the impact she has on the people around her.

According to Travis Bradberry and Jean Greaves, 83 percent of people with high self-awareness are top performers, while only 2 percent of bottom performers display this trait. So self-awareness not only impacts potential, but it also has a direct effect on performance.

Self-awareness can help improve one's career prospects because it makes it easier to understand how others see a leader. This is key for success as it's essential to be aware of the perceptions that the higher-ups have of a leader, but it's also important to know how you come across to your reports and peers when you're working in a leadership capacity.

Empathy:

Before we develop this personality trait we need to understand what empathy means. Most times, we tend to confuse empathy with sympathy. Being empathetic means relating to the feelings another person has regarding a given situation or person. It means being able to understand the needs of the other person, being aware of their feelings and how it impacts their perception. Empathy means you understand what the other person is going through in a given situation.

Empathy enables leaders to provide the required support to move ahead, to deal with the challenges or issues that might be holding them back from achieving their goals.

To start with, leaders need to find the time to become more familiar with the day-to-day issues their subordinates face. Most leaders focus only on getting results from specific engagements that involve their team. Unfortunately, this narrow focus leaves them oblivious to factors that can have an impact on the employee's productivity or ability to complete the assigned tasks.

Contrary to widespread belief, humans by nature are not concerned only with matters of personal gain. Indeed, recent research into mirror neurons has shown that we're wired for sociability and attachment to others and we're driven to connect and understand those we interact with.

If it's part of our make-up to be empathetic and there are also tangible benefits to nurturing a sense of empathy within your organization, then why aren't leaders making empathy a feature of today's business world? The most obvious answer is that any expression of emotion in the workplace is still regarded as a form of weakness and considered unprofessional behaviour. This is another legacy of the industrial age that we have not been able to shun.

Courage:

Aristotle defined courage as the first virtue because it makes all of the other virtues possible. In addition to being the most important virtue in our personal and professional life, it also facilitates other important business deliverables like leadership, innovation, change, expansion, diversification, etc.

Leaders are frequently required to take on audacious targets and often take unpopular decisions, which cannot be done in the absence of courage on their part. Leadership requires the courage to break tradition and convention. Contrary to popular belief, almost everyone can be courageous. Here too the principle of "fake it till you make it" will apply.

Anyone can choose to be courageous. The best way to build courage as a personality trait is to start doing what you are most frightened of. It could be the fear of public speaking, inability to have critical conversations with team members, volunteering ideas in a meeting or any other activity which your role requires. The only way to overcome fear is to do exactly what you are afraid of and that requires courage.

The good news is that with less fear and more courage, workers take on more ambitious projects, deal better with change and speak up more freely about important issues. In short, courageous workers try more, trust more and accomplish more. As a business leader, your job is to be more courageous and create an environment where people can display this trait in abundance.

The traits mentioned above are just a few of the leadership traits that have been identified by experts in this area. The starting point of identifying which personality traits to develop further will be by increasing one's self-awareness. Without self-awareness, leaders will find it very difficult to evolve or to identify traits that need attention.

Being able to tap into one's potential is unlikely unless the leader can accept and overcome blind spots. Simply put, to grow as a leader, one must improve one's ability to recognize and manage one's strongest personality traits while being willing to acknowledge and compensate for one's weaknesses. The leader does not have to go in for a personality transformation, adapting one's behaviour, to meet the requirements of the situation will get her the desired results.

In trying to judge the importance of personality in leadership potential, researchers selected a set of high performers who had the following additional traits and monitored their careers over a period of time to understand who from these sample candidates were high potentials and what were the behavioural traits accountable for their success as leaders.

The traits that the shortlisted group displayed were as follows:

- They were bright
- Outstanding performance record
- Flawed
- Ambitious
- Made many sacrifices for their career

Even people with obvious flaws were not weeded out at this stage and more importance was given to indicators like performance, ambition, willing to make sacrifices for their career for inclusion in likely high potential group.

The personality traits that were found in candidates who did not live up to their assumed leadership potential were:

- Unable to maintain emotional stability
- Poor interpersonal skills
- More focused on advancing own career

- Overconfident and arrogant about own skills
- Defensiveness

Even though the go-getters were expected to do better professionally in the research it was found, being too focused on own career advancement came in the way of candidates living up to their expected potential.

The candidates that did much better professionally displayed slightly different behaviours. What made them successful were the following traits.

- They got along well with all kinds of people.
- They were outspoken but not offensive
- They were perceived as composed under pressure
- Seen to handle mistakes with poise and grace
- They focused on problems and not people.

We may want to check how many of the traits of successful candidates we currently display and create an action plan to master the ones we are not displaying sufficiently

Chapter 6

Potential

"Leadership is unlocking people's potential to become better."

– Bill Bradley

Organizations understand that their employees provide them with a distinct competitive advantage, hence they are committed to hiring, developing and retaining people who display leadership potential. High-potential talent is defined as individuals who possess the leadership capability, business acumen and vision to operate effectively at the next level or successfully take on more responsibilities and grow laterally.

Top companies have an unrelenting focus on the implementation of their leadership-potential policy and this is reflected in their ability to constantly outperform their peers on key financial metrics. The 2014 Aon Hewitt Top Companies for Leaders research found that top-performing companies demonstrated 18% greater return on assets (ROA) and 20% greater return on equity (ROE) over five years when compared to their competitors. These results highlight the importance of leadership potential in driving profitable and business outcomes.

A common misconception is that a high performer is a person with leadership potential, however, this is seldom the case. Just because someone is performing well in their current job role, doesn't mean she will be effective at the next level or perform equally well if given more and different responsibilities.

According to the Human Capital Institute, more than 70% of today's top performers lack the critical characteristics essential for success in future roles. People who perform well in their current positions can fail miserably if they are promoted beyond their level of competence. A high-performing salesperson who hits her target every month isn't guaranteed to have the people skills required as a manager, to train, develop and support others to achieve the same levels of success.

How do you spot leadership potential? What differentiates such an employee from one who has reached a career plateau? Most organizations fall into the trap of relying on current performance as a measure of future potential. Current and past performance may be just one indicator of potential, but the two are not identical.

To tap into one's leadership potential, one must have an honest understanding of who one really is, and what one is capable of accomplishing. Please remember that leadership potential is validated not by the leader herself but by her followers. If they do not trust her or lack confidence in her capabilities, then they will be uninspired by her as a leader. To be successful she has to convince her followers, not herself or her superiors, that she is worthy of being followed.

That is where the four Ps come into play. If your Purpose is not aligned to what you are doing daily or if you are trying to live someone else's dream, there is little likelihood that you will be excelling in your field. If your Performance is not above average consistently people will not look up to you as a leader. If their Perception of your competence, ability to communicate and character is not positive, few people will willingly follow you and your personality also plays an important part in what people perceive you to be.

A leader who wants to stay relevant and effective during her entire work tenure and not reach her level of incompetence will have to reinvent herself repeatedly and will have to move deliberately towards acquiring people management skills and a strategic mind-set. She will have to solicit regular feedback from all stakeholders to gauge how she is scoring on the four Ps. Leadership is not a destination but a journey so this will have to be an ongoing process.

Today organizations do not compete in the marketplace based on the features of their product or service or the price at which the product and/ or service is being offered to the customer. They compete based on the potential of the leaders in the organization and their ability to reinvent themselves as the organization evolves and grows and also their ability to develop more leaders within the organization.

Organizations that can develop more leaders and sooner than the competition will be the future market leaders. Hence one of the most important roles of HR and line managers is to devote time and energy to identifying and developing people who can be groomed as future leaders of the organization.

Research shows that in the Asia Pacific region, 97% of companies that were polled, reported that they have a formal leadership-potential policy in place to identify and groom future leaders, yet just 54% reported that they have an adequate talent pipeline for future leaders for their business. The clear disconnect between intention and outcome demonstrates that simply having a high-potential program is not enough to provide a source of competitive advantage.

As we deal with organizations across industries, we have noticed the same trend where the intent to develop leaders is there but the process is faulty, leading to inconsistent results and disenchanted employees.

Let us see what the organization can do across the four Ps to identify true potential in the organization as developing talent internally is less expensive and safer than acquiring talent from the market.

Purpose: Purpose is something very personal to the employee and an organization does not have much scope to influence it. Is the employee living her dream or someone else's can be observed through the amount of passion she displays for her role. A person with an undefined purpose or a purpose that is different from what she is engaged in does not have much of a chance to be a potential leader in the long term as at some point in time the contradictions will get the better of her. The leader can however try to align the individual's goals to the organizational vision through coaching and mentoring.

Performance: Performance is something that most organizations track, though the majority of them may not be doing a very good job of it. Most performance management systems that I have encountered focus majorly on only one pillar of performance. The system values only the achievement of targets and very little attention is given to how the targets were achieved. The PMS also pays little or no attention to the display of a strategic mind-set and the efforts put into developing talent.

Even tracking the achievement of targets is not sufficient as I have seen teams achieve targets by offering major discounts or dumping products with the dealers before the end of the financial year. As the business exists to make profits by creating satisfied customers, profitability and creating satisfied customers also need to be tracked while evaluating the performance of a leader or a team.

A skewed performance management system will make heroes out of undeserving people and will fail to identify the real contributors to the organization.

Perception: The key to any successful business venture is effective leadership. As leaders with potential are critical to an organization's growth, organizations need to build a sustainable leadership pipeline. Research indicates that 360-degree feedback is one of the most effective methods for developing leaders as it offers an all-round evaluation of the leader and provides a broad view of the leader and their leadership traits. Respondents from a variety of levels in the organization provide feedback on how the individual is perceived.

A 360-degree performance review is a formalized process whereby an employee receives feedback from multiple respondents who regularly engage with the person being reviewed. The objective is to provide the employee with feedback on their performance and behaviours. The respondents typically represent the employee's boss, peers, subordinates and internal and external customers and self.

Self-assessment along with multiple responses from different levels helps the leader identify blind spots and competency gaps. The diversity of viewpoints enables the individual to improve their working relationships and augment their leadership. Highlighting blind spots allows an individual to focus on learning and development needs that apply to those overlooked behaviours.

The 360-degree feedback helps employees in identifying their strengths and an action plan can be created for leveraging the same. Developing strengths is important for an employee's career growth and the company's effectiveness. The output from the 360-degree survey also helps the organization to design individual and group learning initiatives so the L&D resources are utilized optimally.

The 360-degree survey is a very potent tool if utilised well. My experience, however, has been mixed on how effectively this tool is used in most organizations. The things that normally go wrong with the 360-degree survey conducted by most organizations are as under:

- In most cases, it is a 270-degree survey as external customers are seldom included in the survey. It is very important to include internal and external customers in this survey as their point of view is critical in getting the complete picture.

- The selection of respondents has to be done intelligently. The results of the survey can be skewed if the list of the respondent is prepared only by the employee being reviewed, the HR, or the manager as any bias in selecting respondents will defeat the purpose of the survey. All three should select the respondents who will be giving feedback.

- The number of respondents must be sufficiently large so that a couple of respondents cannot influence the results.

In my experience with organizations that we have worked with, they falter on all the three above-mentioned points, whereby the activity does not add real value to the learnings of the person being assessed. For ensuring that all people who have been invited to give feedback HR and line managers will have to pressurise the respondents as most tend not to bother about completing the survey.

Personality: One of the critical elements in ensuring outstanding organisational performance is the selection, development and retention of employees with leadership potential. Research has demonstrated the role that psychometric assessment plays in considerably improving the selection process for both new hires and internal promotions. Inputs from psychometric tests are also used for creating individual and group development plans.

A psychometric test refers to an objective way to measure traits such as aptitude, critical reasoning and behavioural style of the participant. Most psychometric tools also capture how the participant tends to behave under pressure.

Given the high costs of staff turnover and the increased importance of identifying employees who display the aptitude to develop and grow with the organization, psychometric assessment can make a major contribution to talent management.

There are plenty of tests available in the market that help a person get an in-depth understanding of her behavioural makeup. It will help her identify behaviours that can be leveraged to get better outcomes and those that need her to work upon.

As most organizations have their own preferred psychometric tools, I would not like to recommend any. However, I would like to suggest that organizations use this powerful instrument more often to get clarity about the behavioural traits of their employees and for the employees to learn more about their strengths and areas of development.

On many occasions when we are giving feedback to people they tend to get defensive and claim that the findings of the 360- degree report is not an accurate reflection of their true self, but just a perception that people have about them. However, when the psychometric report gives similar insight about the person, they are finally convinced and willing to work on their challenges and leverage their strengths.

I would like to leave the reader with a few thoughts. Firstly, I would urge employees not to look at themselves and others in the organisation as a resource but as talent. Each is unique in its composition and in the way it contributes to the achievement of organizational goals. Talent is something that is not stagnant and can be developed and enhanced. I would also urge managers and leaders to consciously differentiate amongst their team members. The moment you start treating everyone equally, you are not treating true talent fairly. Talent needs to be given preferential treatment by being challenged by ambitious assignments and recognized and rewarded through special treatment.

Secondly, we need to develop better measurement tools for the 21st century. We are still using tools from the industrial age to measure the contribution of employees in the 21st century. I am referring to the Bell Curve where the capability of the team is decided in advance and people are fitted into predetermined slots. This system does not make much of a difference for below-average performers but can be very frustrating for real contributors. HR and the leadership need to come up with a system that rates people based on their true capability and contribution.

Thirdly we need to make the Performance Management System more appropriate. If my task is to fix tyres to brand new cars in the assembly line, then the number of tyres I fix can be a true measure of my performance. However, if I am expected to provide solutions to customers, identify future opportunities and threats, coach mentor and develop my team members, ensure profitability for the organization while addressing the implicit and explicit needs of customers, then evaluating only target achievement may not be the right measure.

I would like to go one step further and suggest that we do away with the performance management system and replace it with a Potential Management System or a Potential Enhancement System. Performance is a post mortem of what has been accomplished while the potential is future-looking and fluid. If the leaders and managers focus on tapping into the potential of the talent that works with them, performance should be a natural outcome of the effort. Potential is not stagnant and focuses on developing and enhancing the capability of the talent available to you.

Investing in the development of talent is the most important and rewarding thing for a leader to engage in, however, it's often the last thing on their "to-do" list as they are busy chasing their monthly and yearly targets. When you develop your team members, they become more productive and perform at a higher level which ultimately makes you successful. Developing employee skills also helps in retaining the best employees and it allows you to delegate so you can focus on your other roles as a manager.

Most importantly developing talent is rewarding because it's what leadership is all about: making a difference in the lives of others and helping them succeed.

www.ingramcontent.com/pod-product-compliance
Lightning Source LLC
Chambersburg PA
CBHW021451210526
45463CB00002B/730